HOW

SEXUAL
HARASSMENT SUIT

...and what to do if you can't!

MARIE,

THANK YOU FOR
YOUR HELP!

ANDY '96

HOW TO AVOID A

SEXUAL
HARASSMENT SUIT

...and what to do if you can't!

Andy Kane

Illustrations by Steve Soeffing

Paladin Press • Boulder, Colorado

How to Avoid a Sexual Harassment Suit
. . . and what to do if you can't!
by Andy Kane

Copyright © 1996 by Andy Kane
ISBN 0-87364-882-X
Printed in the United States of America

Published by Paladin Press, a division of
Paladin Enterprises, Inc., P.O. Box 1307,
Boulder, Colorado 80306, USA.
(303) 443-7250

Direct inquiries and/or orders to the above address.

Illustrations by Steve Soeffing

Contents

Acknowledgments

It's easy to walk away from a person who has problems. When charges or allegations of a moral nature (rape, child molesting, incest, etc.) are made against someone, you probably would not want to invite him to your kid's wedding or hire him as your public relations director. I have personally shunned people over the years who were accused of moral infractions of some sort, and I did it so as not to hurt my business. I regret doing this now, because I had no idea if these people were guilty or not.

This did *not* happen to me when I was accused of sexual harassment; in fact, just the opposite occurred. When the frivolous allegations hit the papers (front page of a paper with a readership of one million) and was the feature story on the six and eleven o'clock news, I received hundreds of encouraging phone calls, letters, and personal visits from past clients, friends, and acquaintances. Some were bank presidents, politicians, columnists, doctors, judges, and other people in highly visible positions. All indicated that they would be willing to testify as a character witness for me, advance funds for attorneys, or help in any way possible. Many past employees called and offered to testify about the working conditions in my office (they were said to be "bizarre" in the lawsuit) or do anything else we needed. I even had an offer from the members of a famous male revue to do a benefit performance to provide funds for our defense! (This group had had sexual harassment charges filed against them even though anyone attending their show would have to know it was a bit risqué.)

One of the most gratifying aspects of all this was that *no one* ever asked if the allegations were true. Obviously, our past dealings with these people had left the impression that I, or any of my staff, would not have done any improper deeds. Roy Forest, the other person accused in the suit, and I are both old, experienced ass-kickers. We never give up without a fight, and we seldom lose, but the added support from these people really helped get our adrenaline flowing.

You never know who your friends are until you need them. All of these people were really great!

The next group of people who really came to our aid were the attorneys and insurance people. The representative from our insurance carrier was the first on the scene and organized the legal and investigative effort. He was a real no-nonsense, get-it-done guy and had a lot of knowledge.

John Belluscio has been our company attorney and my personal attorney for many years, and he supplied advice within minutes of my being served in the suit. He later participated when our insurance carrier sued us. I'm sure John's representation of me over the last decade has taken several years off his life expectancy!

Ron Passero, another attorney I have personally used, represented Roy, but his thorough representation of Roy was very helpful in our defense.

Last but not least is Cheryl Heller, the attorney who represented me and my companies. She was originally assigned to me by the insurance carrier, but later I was given the opportunity to pick my own mouthpiece. I liked the idea of having a female attorney represent me in a sexual harassment case, but I was a bit hesitant. My rear end was on the line, and there was a chance I could lose some real money. I wanted to be sure the lawyer I picked would be a winner.

I had not met Cheryl before I had to select an attorney. All our conversations up to that time had been over the phone because we were both real busy. In my city there are several "bull dyke" type of female attorneys. They dress in men's clothing, and, being a male chauvinist (who else would write a book called *Mastering the Art of Male Supremacy*), I would not be comfortable being represented in court by one of these "ladies." To save time for both of us, I decided to interview Cheryl over the phone. Since I had never seen her, I asked her a few questions designed to rule out my bull dyke fears, and she related that she was married and expecting a child. It had to be the most unusual interview by a potential client she's ever had!

After I satisfied myself she was heterosexual, I asked her about her stature. I was sort of planning on having a 6-foot-tall female attorney who would shout, yell, slam the witness stand, and generally terrorize the plaintiff. Wrong. Cheryl told me she was a petite girl and did not scream and yell in court, though she did impress me that she could get things done and liked to win. I decided to try something new and use her as my attorney. I say something new because until this experience, I had not used women in a professional capacity (I did have my car washed at a topless car wash once, but I'm not sure that counts). I had always had male attorneys, barbers, mechanics, doctors, painters, plumbers, etc. Let me say, using Cheryl was one of the best decisions I ever made! She turned out to be good looking, smart, fun, and very, very aggressive. The opposing attorney was about 6′ 2″, and she pulled his tail, to my delight, more than once.

Another gang that contributed a great deal were the people who worked in our office. Their testimony and recollection of events were amazing. Many were able to repeat conversations word for word, and this was very impressive. Many incidents involving the person who filed the suit were recalled by these people, and without their input, I probably would not have remembered the numerous events.

Now if this was one of those Academy Award acceptance speeches where the winners thank everybody back to the doctor who delivered them, someone probably would have put the hook around my neck by now, but I really want to thank all of the above individuals for their help. This book is dedicated to these great folks and everyone else who came to our aid.

Introduction

First of all let's set the record straight. I am not a lawyer. I don't look like a lawyer. I don't smell like a lawyer. I don't own a funny-looking three-piece suit! This book is *not* to be used in place of a lawyer, and any advice should not be construed as legal advice. I'm just a hard-working high school graduate (top half of the lower third of my class) who owns some apartment houses and two real estate companies in a large city in western New York state. I work very hard for my money, go to the job each day, and have all the same obligations as you do. I have worked continuously at many occupations since I was 14 years old. I have amassed a good-sized portfolio of property, and my two real estate businesses are well established. All this has taken more than 40 years of real hard work, and I started with zilch. I am not the type of boss who sends a crew over to a dilapidated property and tells them to fix it up—I go with them. I have supervised and actually worked—pick and shovel, broom, paint brush, saw, hammer, and other real dirty work—on *every* project I have ever been involved with. My usual attire is jeans and a T-shirt, and by closely supervising and actually physically working on each renovation or construction job, I have been able to turn some ugly ducklings into swans for thousands of dollars less than if I had contracted the entire job out.

But the goal of this book is not to tell you how to make a million bucks in real estate by rehabbing slums. I think there are already a few hundred books available on late night TV to guide you through that field. (The best one by far is entitled ". . . And This Is the Bathroom": How to Really Sell Real Estate by Andy Kane, also available from Paladin Press.) The goal of this book is to help you keep the money that you have already earned or will earn through your years of hard work!

Over the past few years, the feminazis* of our country, quietly and little by little, have built a spider web of nasty little laws, ordinances, and regulations to trap innocent males* and suck their life savings out of them. This book will at least make you aware of some of the schemes and traps that are used by these feminazis to harass the good-old boys who are out making our economy work. By being aware of things you do that can be considered sexual harassment instead of friendliness or politeness, you *may* be able to avoid having your name on a lawsuit or on the front page of the daily fish wrapper.

You may wonder why I took time from my busy life of selling homes, evicting helpless tenants, renovating slums, and vacationing in exotic locals with my beautiful bride to research and write a book about sexual harassment. Well, it's really not uncommon for me to write a book or two (actually this is my seventh) to help my fellow man make it through this treacherous life.

---

* From time to time you will encounter this asterisk symbol. This indicates that the meaning of these terms can be found in the glossary at the end of the book.

Secretary's suit alleges harassment

Real estate agent accused of fondling

By J. Leslie Sopko

Democrat and Chronicle

A Webster woman is seeking $3.5 million in a sexual harassment lawsuit filed against real estate agent Andy Kane, alleging she was exposed to "outrageous and bizarre acts," including the unwanted touching of her breasts.

▓▓▓▓▓▓▓▓▓▓, a former typist at Andy Kane Realty Corp., said in a lawsuit that she was given an employee handbook written by Kane called *Mastering the Art of Male Supremacy.*

Kane's book gives tips to men on how to keep a wife in line: "I don't condone violence — maybe a rolled up newspaper on the rump once in awhile — but no real violence. Besides violence is not the best way. It only worked for the cavemen because there were no alternate methods back in those ' the book states.

So why did I suddenly decide on this subject? Was it the Clarence Thomas/Anita Hill hearing that monopolized the TV for weeks? Nope. I had a secretary retire after 20 or so years in my office, and I placed an ad for a replacement in the paper. A girl about 20 years old answered the ad and presented me with a very impressive résumé. I agreed to give her a shot at the job and contracted for her services on a temporary basis with the idea of hiring her full-time if she worked out.

Needless to say, her résumé contained a few exaggerations, her work was less than satisfactory, and her mistakes were beginning to cause big problems to the people in the office and my clients. So we parted company.

After the girl left, some semblance of order returned to my office. I hired another temporary secretary and I expected to never see or hear from this person again.

Several months later, the newspaper that serves our city had its annual fund raiser for charity. It's a sale of newspapers on busy downtown street corners. Local businessmen dress up in costumes and try to out-do each other in volume of sales. The proceeds are then donated to a local charity. The businessmen donate their time, and the event has produced hundreds of thousands of dollars for worthy causes. I have done this every year for more than 20 years. I have been on the same corner every year, and everyone knows where to look for me. I'm always in the middle of Broad and Fitzhugh Streets wearing a huge 3-foot-high orange cowboy hat!

People pull up, hand me money, and get a paper. Some people give $10, $20, $50, and even $100 for just one paper! I'm always quick to put my hand out when a car stops. Along comes this black four-door sedan with one well-dressed male driving. It slows down, I put out my hand expecting a $5, $10, or $20, and instead I got a subpoena for a $14 million lawsuit claiming sexual harassment by the girl we had dismissed! The dude in the black sedan was a process server! It almost makes you never want to do anything good again. The suit named me, a manager of one of my real estate companies, and both real estate companies—sort of a shotgun approach hoping to hit somebody or some company with money.

I won't go into the details of that frivolous suit now, but at least you have an idea of what prompted me to again sit down and scribble off important book number seven. I hope it helps you and my fellow man.

Nice country we live in. God bless America!

1. What Is Sexual Harassment?

That's a good question, but before I define sexual harassment let me tell you about a problem I had in the tenth grade about 40 years ago. The name of that problem was algebra (x squared $- 4\,y$ = something or other). I never could master that subject. I didn't even come close to understanding it, and to make things even worse, my teacher, Mr. Byrnes, told us that unless we completely and thoroughly understood algebra we would *never* amount to anything! We would not even get a job on an ash wagon. (For you young whippersnappers who are unfamiliar with ash wagons, let me illustrate. In the old days, homes were heated by coal or wood, the residue was ashes, and they had to be hauled away to the dump by a horse and wagon. The ashes were loaded on these wagons by nitwits who were about two stages dumber than the horses that pulled the wagon, and it was about the dirtiest, lowest-paying job in the world.)

Well, I left high school with my tail between my legs, having flunked algebra and expecting the world to pounce on me because I didn't know how much x squared $- 4$ was. But I quickly learned that there was life after

algebraic death. I found various jobs above the ash gang standard. Many were in the engineering field, and I obtained patents for various inventions. I also purchased apartment buildings, wrote books, and sold cars, real estate, and various other things. Incidentally, in 30 years of selling these and other extremely high-ticket items, I have never had a buyer tell me he had x squared, 3 y, and n to the fourth power as a down payment! Several did tell me they had five g's, and I learned that a "g" was short for a grand, and that a grand was short for one thousand good old American bucks! That's the only algebra I needed to make a good living and support myself, my beautiful wife, and my two stinkin' kids.

What this story illustrates is that you can get along in life without completely understanding every subject that someone tries to cram down your throat, and for the last decade or so, the feminazis have tried to cram sexual harassment, or their version of imagined sexual harassment, down our throats.

I'm now going to describe several common crimes that occur in our cities every day so that a comparison can be made between these well-documented offenses and the dreaded sexual harassment crime.

MURDER

I find out my lady is getting her bones jumped by the milkman. I do not want to harm the little lady, because then my dirty socks and dishes will start to pile up. I wait in the bushes with my 20-gauge shotgun and when the milkman climbs out of the bedroom window, I send his skull into the next pasture.

Now this is murder. How do we know it? 1) There is a victim. There is *absolutely* no doubt in the victim's mind (or what's left of it) that he is a victim. 2) There is a perpetrator, and that perpetrator *absolutely* knows he committed a crime. There can be no doubt in his mind that he committed a dastardly deed. 3) There is evidence . . . hard, physical, visible evidence (gun, shell, body, blood, scattered milk bottles, etc.).

CAR THEFT

You need a loaf of bread, so you stop at the corner convenience store and run in. Since you are only going to be inside for about 30 seconds, you leave the car running. I'll bet you can guess the rest. A bored, underprivileged, abused youth who has had a very, very unhappy childhood and has never had the opportunity to drive a sparkling new Cadillac like yours cannot resist this golden opportunity to raise his social status. As you are paying for your bread, you hear tires squeal and see your car disappear down the avenue. Several hours later, after a few minor accidents and a police chase, the misguided youth is apprehended.

This is a car theft. How do we know it? 1) There is a victim. The victim has *absolutely* no doubt that he is a victim. His car is gone, he saw it go, and he had to walk home. He will have to pay the $100 deductible before he can get his fenders banged back out. He is a victim. 2) There is a perpetrator, and the perpetrator *absolutely* knows he committed a crime. He saw the running car unattended. He planned and executed the theft. It was not his car, and he made precise physical moves to jump in and drive away. There can be absolutely no doubt in his mind that he committed a dastardly deed. 3) There is evidence . . . hard, physical, visible evidence (fingerprints, damaged cars, $100 less for your groceries this week, etc.).

CONVENIENCE STORE STICKUP

The bored, underprivileged, abused youth who has had a very, very, unhappy childhood could not find a car in the store parking lot with the keys in it, so he enters the store, smiles at the security video camera, whips out a long, sharp knife and tells the 16-year-old pimply faced clerk to give him all the money in the cash register or he will need all the Band-Aids in the store. The clerk complies and the robber flees.

This is an armed robbery. How do we know it? 1) There is a victim. The victim has *absolutely* no doubt that he is a victim (since he probably peed his pants when he saw the knife). 2) There is a perpetrator, and that perpetrator *absolutely* knows he committed a crime. He armed himself with the knife, went to the store, made precise physical moves to draw the weapon, and made the demand for money. There can be *absolutely* no doubt in his mind that he committed this dastardly deed. 3) There is evidence . . . hard, physical, visible evidence (video camera tape, wet spot on floor near register, etc.).

SEXUAL HARASSMENT

You are a male administrator at a large hospital in upstate New York. You are going to take a trip to New York City in the near future, and you ask a female assistant administrator to join you on this trip. She declines and says that she is married. You ask, "Have you heard of open marriages?" A year or so later, you, the hospital, and your boss are named in a $200,000 sexual harassment lawsuit!

Is this sexual harassment? How would you know it? 1) Is there a victim? Evidently the female recipient of the invitation feels she is a victim or she wouldn't have filed the suit. (I'm sure it couldn't have anything to do with the 200,000 U.S. bucks.) You probably have heard the old saying, "Beauty is in the eye of the beholder." Well the feminazis seem to have rearranged this saying to, "Sexual harassment is in the eye of the beholder." 2) Is there a perpetrator? Does he know he committed a dastardly deed? Think about this. Have you ever asked a female to accompany you to New York City (or Philadelphia, Trenton, Sandy Hook, Miami, Daytona, Toronto, Paris,

Chappaquiddick, etc.)? Did she say, "No, I'm married" (or working that day, doing my laundry, shopping, etc.). And did you ever answer with a snappy comeback like, "Tell your old man you are going to see a 'sick aunt' (or a Mets game, the opera, a play, etc.)."

In most cases of sexual harassment, the alleged perpetrator *does not have any idea* that he has committed the dastardly act. In the case of the murder, car theft, and stickup, the perpetrator absolutely knew from the get-go that he was committing a crime. There are guidelines, laws, and ordinances that determine where everyday activities stop and a crime begins for just about everything in the world *except* sexual harassment. Sexual harassment is generally considered to be any word, act, event, occurrence, deed, object, picture, smell, taste, color, look, touch, temperature, style, dress, or undress that someone *feels* is harassing to her! Some guidelines! To make it even more complicated, you do not even have to be the person harassed by the actions to file a complaint. That's right! If you are in an environment where sexual harassment is occurring and it's not directed at you but you feel affected by it and it makes you uncomfortable, you can file charges!

There is an old story that says that "close" only counts in horseshoes and hand grenades. I think this saying may have to be revised to include sexual harassment.

As you can see, it is very difficult to define what sexual harassment is. I would say that this offense has been committed by everyone of us, regardless of sex or age, at one time or another. Think back. Have you ever placed your hand on your secretary's shoulder to get her attention? Have you ever hung a calendar in your office or place of business that could be considered objectionable? Have you ever told an off-color joke? Have you ever wolf-whistled at the mail girl? Have you ever complimented a n office worker on her great anatomy? Have you ever suggested that you and any member of the opposite sex

$1M award for harassment

The Associated Press

A man who said his female boss fondled him and made threats after he rejected her advances was awarded $1 million by Los Angeles jurors in a sexual harassment lawsuit.

Sabino Gutierrez, 33, claimed he was sexually harassed almost daily for six years by Maria Martinez, chief financial officer and director of personnel of Cal Spas, a hot tub manufacturer.

"My case is a perfect example of a company that didn't listen to my complaints and as a result they will pay a very high price for ignoring the situation," the Ontario, Calif., man said yesterday, a day after a Superior Court jury awarded the damages.

The company said it was considering an appeal. Mary Maloney Roberts, an attorney for the Pomona company, said Martinez denied harassing Gutierrez.

could have a good time together? Never done any of this, you say? The confessional is open every Saturday at Saint What's-His-Name—you better get over there and tell Father O'Brien that you are a liar!

You say you are gay and you don't have to worry? Guess what! You do not have to be of the opposite sex to have sexual harassment charges filed against you. Charges can be girl to girl or guy to guy.

I have heard of charges that have destroyed careers of 30 years or more, and such charges can come at any time and in any occupation. Most are based upon the alleged victims *interpretation* of the alleged perpetrator's remarks or actions, with no regard as to what the alleged perpetrator actually intended to convey by his remarks or actions.

Have I answered the question, "What is sexual harassment?" I doubt it. I don't believe you can get a black and white answer, because the guidelines are not black and white. As long as the alleged victim is the one who is allowed to define sexual harassment, it is unlikely that anyone will be able to define it.

I would suggest one definition, and that is "legal blackmail." Although you may have read about hundreds of cases in the papers, that is just the tip of the iceberg. The cases you read about are the ones where the accused resists the offer to settle quietly and without fanfare. Even the Clarence Thomas case could have been avoided if he would have withdrawn from the Supreme Court nomination process, but he chose to stand his ground and I congratulate him on his hard decision. I hope it gives others the courage to stand their ground when they know they are right and to not fall victim to the legalized blackmail of sexual harassment. When someone takes the easy way out, this encourages the person who accused him to try it again on another person or business for another windfall, and this process will be on-going until someone she accuses digs in his heels and says, "Go to hell!" and breaks her money chain.

Let me get something straight. I in no way condone *real* sexual harassment, and I define *real* sexual harassment as:

1. *A direct request by a boss for sex from an employee*, with loss of job the prize for a "no" answer.

2. *Continued requests for sex from fellow employees.* By continual I mean more than three or four times. I think once or twice, in a nice romantic way, is okay. If you rule out any requests for dates or sex, I think you are going against the plan the big man upstairs has for us to replenish the supply of people on this earth.

3. *Requiring unusual dress codes.* I say unusual because every job is different. If you own a topless bar, you cannot allow the dancers to wear turtleneck sweaters. The dress code has to be revealing and sexy or the place will go bust! If you run a business office, you should at least be able to ask your employees to look businesslike.

4. *Inconsiderate working conditions.* But working conditions should be considerate of *both* sexes. If men want a pin-up calendar in the men's locker room, OK. In the main lobby or offices frequented by ladies, probably not. I say "probably not" because the type of establishment may dictate a sexy calendar in the lobby. Take, for an example, an auto salvage yard, auto parts wholesaler, or plumbing and heating supply store. Most tool and parts manufacturers supply the outlets with girlie calendars, and most are very tasteful and important advertising tools.

5. *Touching/grabbing/feeling.* Definitely a no-no. I cannot think of any legal business where this can be tolerated. A mutual hug here or there could easily be acceptable since many ethnic groups consider the hug equivalent to a handshake. If the huggee is screaming and trying to stab the hugger with a letter opener, then I would not consider this to be a mutually agreed upon hug.

I believe these are the limits, and they are based upon *common sense*. Speaking of common sense, an associate of mine suggested that the term is a misnomer. He said that since so many people today lack common sense, on the uncommon occasion when someone says something that in the past would be considered common sense, it should be referred to as uncommon sense!

Until definite parameters are set by law, we are going to have many careers ruined, many rich lawyers, much valuable court time devoted to frivolous lawsuits, and very strained relationships between the sexes.

I am now going to tell you about a real sexual harassment complaint that my company received shortly after the multimillion dollar complaint was filed by the ex-secretary.

One day, the manager of my rental company received a call from a female claiming that she had been sexually harassed by one of our agents. The manager immediately asked me to pick up another phone so we could both evaluate this new charge. We listened intently as the girl described what had happened the day before.

First, let me describe how our rental service works. A landlord hires us to find a tenant for a vacant or soon-to-be-vacant apartment. He gives us the keys, and we show the unit, check out the prospective tenant, and collect the first month's rent. Sometimes the apartment is occupied, so then we call to let the existing tenant know we will be showing the unit.

In this case the tenant was home but elected not to answer the phone. She also did not respond to the knock on the door when our agent, Jerry, arrived. Jerry used the key supplied by the landlord and the door opened 4 inches, just the length of the security chain the tenant had on the door. She then came to the door and Jerry told her the reason for his attempted entry. She indicated that he would have to come back another time to show the prospective tenant the unit, so Jerry left.

After she described the above event to us, I asked several questions trying to determine where the sexual harassment occurred. I asked:

Q: Were you dressed when you came to the door?

A: Yes, fully dressed.

Q: Did Jerry say something off-color?

A: No, it was nothing he said.

Q: Miss, did he do or say something that upset you?

A: No. It was *the way he looked at me!*

Through a 4-inch opening, he looked at her in a sexually harassing way. Can you believe this! A look!

I replied, so as not to offend this girl, "We will certainly take care of this right away, and I guarantee it will never happen again!" That seemed to satisfy her, and that's the last we ever heard about it.

Let me tell you a little about Jerry. He's middle aged, is happily married to a real nice lady, has one kid, takes frequent vacations with his family, is retired from a major film-making company and is, a very stable, polite individual. Not what I would consider your regular, everyday sexual harasser.

How did we solve this horrendous, terrible, life-threatening problem? Let's see how you would have handled it!

❑ Fire Jerry.
❑ Suspend Jerry.
❑ Counsel Jerry.
❑ Forget the whole deal.
❑ Ask Jerry to wear sunglasses when showing
    apartments.

If you marked the last box, you hit the nail on the head. Obviously the imagination of the accuser was running wild, but I believe some companies would have fired Jerry to appease the accuser since they would be worried about a lawsuit.

If you think the Jerry story is way out there, let me throw another one at you. At what age do you think sexual harassment begins? The youngest case I have run across occurred in Minnesota. That's right, Minnesota, where nothing ever happens. Not New York City, New Jersey, Philadelphia, or some high-density metropolitan area, but Minnesota! I don't even know where it is!

Here's the story. A mother in Eden Prairie, Minnesota, filed sexual harassment charges with the human rights commission claiming that the little boys on her *7-year-old* daughter's school bus were sexually harassing her daughter! The co-president of the Eden Prairie school district thought that possibly the mother was "overreacting." The school superintendent also indicated that Minnesota law had recently been changed to allow money to be recovered for sexual harassment. Can you imagine how the outcome of this will affect the 7-year-old's social life? Can you see a little boy ever asking her to the kindergarten prom? I am sure this mother has done

Judge allows girl's suit over alleged abuse in sixth grade

THE ASSOCIATED PRESS

ALBANY — A teen can sue over the alleged failure of school officials to stop her from being insulted and touched by male classmates in the sixth grade, a federal judge has ruled.

Federal Judge Thomas J. McAvoy upheld virtually all of a suit that a lawyer is trying to bring on behalf of 13-year-old Eve Bruneau against the South Kortright school district, in Delaware County, about 65 miles west of Albany.

The teen, who has since transferred to the nearby Stamford school district, claims the complaints she and other girls made about the behavior of boys were ignored. The girl was denied equal protection under the law, her suit claims.

The suit seeks unspecified damages. Eve's attorney Merrick T. Rossein, a Queens lawyer and expert on sex discrimination cases, called on the district to settle out of court. If not, he predicted that a jury will agree with Eve's contentions.

According to the suit, Eve's sixth-grade teacher, William Parker Jr., allowed boys to kick, touch and hit girls, snap their bra straps and refer to them as "bitch" and "lesbian." Complaints by Eve and other girls did not stop the problems, the suit says.

The U.S. Supreme Court ruled two years ago that students can sue for harassment, as adults can for harassment in the workplace. Rossein contends the South Kortright situation is a violation of federal Title IX, a 1972 federal law designed to enforce gender equity.

District officials argue that Parker did act to protect the girls from misbehaving boys and that a case made on the basis of a federal law against workplace gender harassment is not suitable to a classroom full of young students.

"Adults in the workplace are a little bit more responsible than 12-year-olds in a schoolhouse," said Frank Miller, a lawyer for the district.

Pat Schofield, Eve's mother, said she was "ecstatic" at McAvoy's ruling, which was handed down on Tuesday.

"But it seems like they (district officials) still don't get it," she told the *Oneonta Daily Star*. "They don't get that this is real."

McAvoy has not yet set a trial date. The suit names the district and the school board. ❑

more harm than good. Again, this sexual harassment deal is being used to put some bucks in someone's pocket and not to punish real sexual harassers.

Since there are no limits on age for sexual harassment complaints, can you see this: the new mother looks through the window of the nursery in the hospital several hours after the birth of her baby girl. The little darling is just lying there in the basket enjoying her first hours of life on our planet. The mother happens to glance over at the next basket and to her dismay she discovers a little boy licking his lips and looking at her daughter! My gosh, this is certainly a prime case of sexual harassment! (It couldn't be that our little boy is having gas pains or whatever these little urchins have at that age.) Have no doubt that someone will go this far unless rules are cast in stone.

What about upper limits on age? My mother is in her nineties and in a nursing home. I see many old geezers, strapped in wheelchairs, unable to move much more than their noggins. I have heard, "Hey beautiful," and other comments from these members of the senior citizen set. If a person decided to file a complaint, I'm sure it would get the same attention as the complaint from the 7-year-old on the school bus. These two conditions may seem unreal, but they are certainly possible, and as more people reap windfall bucks from sexual harassment scams, you may read about similar situations in the daily news.

Men charging men with sexual harassment has also made the news and talk shows on many occasions. On one nationwide talk show, a social worker in California revealed how he was harassed at work by a guy. He said, "It was not uncommon for any of us to go off to talk with our supervisors. A year ago, he drove me to an isolated area. I said, 'Well, what do you want to talk about?' He lit up a marijuana joint, and his whole facial expression changed. This man weighs 300 to 400 pounds, and he said, 'Trust me.' He turned to me and he groped me and he tried to kiss me. I pushed him off. I said, 'Get out of here!' He got out of the car, walked over to the passenger side where the window was down on my side, and said, 'I'm going to have you or I'm going to kill you.' I jumped out of the car and walked five miles to a phone and called a friend. I reported the harassment to his superiors, but no charges were filed. My supervisor who harassed me was sent on a vacation and I was transferred."

There are numerous other situations where men have accused men of sexual harassment. Many have occurred in the United States and Canadian military, but a famous one was when the ex-host of the TV show "Dance Fever," Deney Terrio, filed a sexual harassment case against the media mogul/casino owner Merv Griffin. Do you think if

NEW YORK

Elevator eyes are a no-no, Assembly members warned

The Associated Press

ALBANY — New York state Assembly members, ordered by their boss to learn how to prevent sexual harassment, listened to an hour-long lecture yesterday about "elevator eyes" and legal liability.

The mandatory seminar came two months after a former Assembly staff member testified at a public hearing that sexual harassment was widespread at New York's state Capitol.

"After the Anita Hill-Clarence Thomas hearings, times have changed," Francine Moccio, director of the Cornell University Institute on Women and Work told the lawmakers. "It is a different playing field and we have to watch what we say."

That means curbing sexual jokes and avoiding elevator eyes — ogling a person from head to toe, she said.

It also means added responsibilities as supervisors. That appeared

to concern some of the politicians who went through yesterday's training.

"I really hadn't realized the level of liability all up the line," said Assemblyman Arthur Eve of Buffalo.

Meanwhile, a task force appointed by Gov. Mario Cuomo recommended yesterday that all employers in New York be required to institute a policy that prohibits sexual harassment. Companies should also be forced to run their own training seminars, the task force said.

The report came from the task force that heard from former Assembly employee Charmain Neary in September. She said her ex-boss, former Assemblyman Mark Alan Siegel, "introduced sex into almost every encounter with women" and said his behavior wasn't unusual in Albany. Siegel has denied the charges. ◻

22

Griffin was a 40-hour-a-week factory worker instead of a well-known millionaire, Terrio would have bothered to file a suit? I doubt it.

A good example of the difficulty in defining sexual harassment arose when all New York state assembly members were ordered to attend sensitivity classes on sexual harassment after a female staff member of an assemblyman complained that sexual harassment was widespread in the state capitol. Evidently these well-educated lawmakers, most of whom were attorneys, were unable to interpret the maze of laws that made up the sexual harassment section. Can you imagine—the lawmakers had to have a seminar so that they could see what they were doing wrong! Many were surprised to discover that elevator eyes were grounds for sexual harassment charges (see Associated Press article).

Pretty soon we will have to attend classes to train our eyes to look straight ahead and never down for fear we may offend someone. Even the old milk wagon horses with their blinders were allowed to look up and down. The blinders only prevented them from looking side to side.

Sexual harassment is nearly impossible to define, but the best thing you can do is to keep your eyes and ears open when around any person or event that you feel uncomfortable with. It's better to be safe than sorry.

2. Targets

Have you seen those lovely greeting cards available every year at Valentines's Day where Cupid is shooting his love arrow at an unsuspecting male? There should be a similar card for the feminazis who use sexual harassment as a money maker. The card would show a feminazi aiming at the back of an unsuspecting male. On his rump

would be a target: bull's-eye = $10 million, next ring = $8 million, next = $7 million, etc. It would be a big seller!

In this chapter I am going to tell you about targets. It's pretty easy to define who might or might not be a target. It's certainly easier than defining what is and is not sexual harassment. You can almost use the same system that's used to define possible heart attack victims—i.e., personality type A is most likely to have his ticker quit. Instead, we are going to rate possible targets as you would lovely ladies in a beauty contest: 1 through 10, with bonus points available for certain traits (friendly, outgoing, complimentary, etc.). Let's rate some target occupations . . .

SPORTS STARS

If you are an athlete who is well known nationally or locally or even retired from active participation in sports but still maintains a high-profile life-style, you can easily be a target. When someone accuses you, it will make headlines, and the accuser will get all sorts of instant gratification and also contaminate potential jurors who read of the allegations in the papers, which may well lead to a monetary verdict in favor of the feminazi who filed the charges.

Sports can be a very dangerous profession—race car drivers get killed or injured on the track; football players can suffer disabling injuries on the field; boxers get punchy in the ring; hockey players get slammed, sticked, and punched on the rink; basketball players get fouled, elbowed, and gouged on the court. As a result, all these athletes may feel safe as they walk off the court or track, but that is where the danger really begins! You cannot be sued for sexual harassment for your actions on the field or court (I hope). It's when you go to your hotel room, press party, or victory dinner where the real threat (to your wallet) lurks. If you

happen to put your arm around the waist of a well-wisher or accept a hug from an admirer, it may be recorded on a cameraman's videotape. Although it was an innocent gesture at the time, when the jury sees this tape you will appear to be "Freddy the Fondler."

This profession rates an 8.

CAR SALESMEN

You probably have heard people talk about car salesmen in the same category as ambulance-chasing lawyers, but keep in mind that every time this guy sells a shiny new sedan, our economy moves ahead a little bit. The Detroit assembly line moves one car length, the lug nut twisters and carburetor installers take home a paycheck, the truck driver delivering the new sedan earns a buck or two, the dealership makes some profit, and many other hundreds of people in between benefit from the car salesman's ability.

To be good car salesman, a man must be good at dealing with people. He must be outgoing. He must compliment the lady looking at the car. He must charm her or she will move on to the next dealer's lot. He may even take a test drive with her, all alone, just the two of them, and many test drives are on lonesome roads to avoid heavy traffic. The potential for being accused is great. She is

driving and says, "Where are the wipers?" He reaches across her and points them out. His arm or hand touches her arm, leg, or boob. She makes the deal and gets the wagon for 10 bucks over sticker. Monday she drives to work and sees her girlfriend with the exact same car! That's worse than two girls showing up at the dance with the same dress, but the kicker comes when she finds out that her girlfriend got her jalopy for only 5 bucks over sticker!

Obviously she does what every red-blooded feminazi would do. She files a lawsuit against the salesman and the dealership for $20 million! The charge is not for losing 5 bucks more on the deal but for sexual harassment! The salesman took her out on a lonely road and touched her leg.

Car salesman gets a 6.

TEACHERS OR PROFESSORS

You probably will be all right in front of the entire class, but if I were still teaching I would *never* keep one opposite-sex student after class. You don't keep a good student after class; the one you keep is the one who is having problems. If she is having a problem, she may think that her problem is the result of your attitude, your ability as a teacher, or your prejudice against her. If you confine this possibly hostile student in a room alone with you, you are asking for trouble. Although your motive may have been excellent, this student may seek revenge for having been given a poor grade or reprimand and file a charge of sexual harassment against you. One solution is to make it a policy to have a witness present any time you must keep a student after school. This will greatly reduce your risk of being accused of something you did not do.

We are going to grade teachers or professors on a curve: grammar school 2, high school 5, college 7.

ENTERTAINERS

Entertainers face much the same risks as jocks, only increased due to the effect that groupies have on this profession. Many stars have to travel incommunicado, use disguises, or have bodyguards just to keep women or girls from throwing their luscious bodies at them. (Tough life!) Many female fans chase after their favorite star and will even travel to distant cities to see him perform or to visit his home. Some have actually broken into stars' residences or torn the clothes off their bodies. This is not something new. These crazy chicks have been around since the 1930s. Even "Old Blue Eyes" had his problem with women throwing themselves at him.

There are parties in hotel rooms when group sex is offered, occurs, or is imagined and ends up on the front page of the scandal magazine at the grocery store

Sex suit stuns 'Wonder Years' stars

"Wonder Years" star Fred Savage is shocked and shaken by a lawsuit from a pretty wardrobe assistant who claims she was sexually harassed by Fred and costar Jason Hervey.

Monique Long, 31 — pictured for the first time exclusively in The ENQUIRER — filed suit in Los Angeles on March 15, charging she's suffered "extreme mental anguish" because of sexual harassment from Fred, 16, and 20-year-old Jason.

But sources close to the show insist the two stars are innocent victims of a vindictive ex-employee who was fired from the show last October.

Fred moaned to a "Wonder Years" insider: "I feel like someone kicked me in the stomach for no reason. I just don't understand why Monique decided to go after Jason and me like that."

SHAKEN Fred Savage (right) and Jason Hervey film last episode of "Wonder Years."

And Fred told a set source: "This suit mess has really gotten to me. I've been muffing my lines like never before. I can't seem to concentrate.

"This crazy girl and her false allegations are keeping me up nights. I can't sleep. I keep thinking, 'Why me?' "

Monique's suit claims Fred repeat-

'This crazy girl & her false allegations are keeping me up nights'

edly made sexual remarks to her and attempted "such unwelcomed touchings" as holding her hand and "persistently asking her to have an affair with him."

And she charges that last August, Jason grabbed her by the arms from behind and "pretended as if he were having sex with her."

But the set source declared: "Monique is a vindictive shrew to go after Fred and Jason this way.

"Fred told me, 'Many of the show's fans look on my character Kevin Arnold as a real pal. They grew up with this show just like I did. And when something like this comes along, you wonder how it will affect the audience's view of Kevin.

" 'I want to tell everyone: Hey, don't worry — I'm innocent!' "

— JANE LIEBERMAN

20

checkout. If you do partake in one of the orgies, you may find out later that the girl who was crawling all over you for two hours has now accused you of sexual harassment! This is not uncommon. When she was rubbing herself up and down your great body, she thought you were going to fall in love with her and she would live happily ever after on your Beverly Hills estate. When this did not occur and you left her there for the roadies to play with, she suddenly decides that you enticed her there (even though she probably had to climb the fire escape to get past your security people) and sexually harassed her.

Obviously you have big bucks, are famous, and are usually older than the offended female, so the accusations will be on hundreds of front pages and TV screens. I'm sure you have read of many cases just like this, but the sad thing is, many people who are accused simply pay the accuser off to avoid bad publicity and you never hear about it!

This really does not work. The legalized blackmail just continues. The girl who scores with a grand payoff tells another girl, who arranges a chance meeting with the vulnerable entertainer and later files her suit. Since girl #1 got $50,000, girl #2 uses that as a benchmark and insists on $75,000 for her traumatic experience. This can go on and on. The bigger the entertainer, the more the risk.

It's always surprised me that Elvis has not had a sexual harassment complaint against him since his reported death. There have been so many reported sightings of Elvis, I'm surprised one of the females who has spotted him has not said that he fondled her as she was waiting in line at the Burger King. The terrible thing is, if this really happened, Graceland would probably pay off to keep Elvis' reputation intact!

I am going to give entertainers an adjustable rating also. If you are the lead guitarist for the Skillet Lickers and play every Wednesday night at a roadhouse in Louisiana, I would give

you a 1. If you are an Elvis-caliber entertainer, you rate a 9.5, and if you are somewhere in between, give it a good guess.

APPLIANCE SERVICEMEN
(also heating, plumbing, and electric servicemen and phone and cable TV repairmen who make house calls)

Why do we consider the guys who replace dishwasher regurgitaters? Many times these guys find themselves in a house with a bored housewife. She may be clad in anything from a towel to a bikini, slip, sheer nightgown, or undies. I'm sure this would not entice me (my wife might read this book!), but many guys aren't made of the same moral stuff that I am. Some don't care if they get AIDS, and some just don't care about anything.

A sort of reverse psychology will be used here. If the lady of the house comes on to you and you jump her bones, you may never hear from her again. You have been bad, but that's good. If you are good and say, "No thanks, I got one of those at home," that's bad. You have turned this lady down, and ladies do not like that. Sometimes they seek revenge, and sexual harassment allegations are common when two people get together in a house and one does not get what she wants.

There is not much you can do to protect yourself, but you can use caution. If a situation seems to be leading to something that does not interest you, get out fast. Your leaving will possibly discourage her from complaining.

Your chances of being approached are based upon several things here. Are you a good-looking stud like me or are you fat and bald? Is your company a big, well-known, national corporation or a small mom-and-pop deal? Is your service vehicle shiny, new, and expensive, or does it look like my plumber's truck, which he rolled over several years ago and banged back out with a pipe wrench? If you are good looking, have a nice vehicle, and work for a big, well-known company, you will be a better target than my 5-foot-tall, 300-pound plumber with the rolled-over truck.

This one gets a 6. (My plumber gets a -2.)

POLITICIANS
(including candidates for
any office or government position)

Anita Hill ambushing Clarence Thomas is probably the most publicized and promoted sexual harassment case in history. Here was a guy whose public image was virtually spotless. He had been on the appeals court in the nation's capitol and had been the top decision maker at a large federal agency for several years. He was the number one black neoconservative in the Reagan administration. He had been investigated by the FBI and confirmed by the United States Senate four times for various positions. That he'd survived innumerable hearings meant that there was not much left to find. Here was Mr. Clean.

Yet he made a perfect target for Hill as she told her story of sexual harassment. When did the alleged harassment occur? In 1981, nearly *10* years before his confirmation hearings! Even if you fudge on your tax return, the IRS doesn't grab you after 10 years. Luckily for America, justice prevailed in the Thomas case, and this man took his rightful place on the Supreme Court. Here was a guy who was squeaky clean, checked out by the FBI, and a sexual harassment claim *still* nearly ruined him.

How about Chappiquiddick Ted? His family has prestige, money, and power. Not only is Ted a perfect candidate for sexual harassment charges, everyone in his

family are excellent targets. (Remember the William Kennedy Smith case in Florida?) When you are in politics, you have added exposure because your opposition will turn over every rock to find something to rub your nose in.

If they can't find something in your past, they will not hesitate to create a situation. It's interesting to note that when U.S. Senator Bob Packwood of Oregon was charged with sexual harassment, 15 women came forward simultaneously to bring the charges into the open. Suddenly we have 15 feminists coming forward to be martyrs at once. One interesting aspect is that some had been former members of Packwood's party but now were employed by the opposition. Some of the alleged actions occurred in 1969, 23 years before the offended women came forward. Can you remember the events of 1969? That's one hell of a long time to hold a grudge. Incidentally, the accused senator was a friend of the feminist movement and supported many feminist causes. If they do this to a friend, can you imagine what they would and can do to an enemy? The old saying certainly applies: "With friends like this, who needs enemies."

You have to be on guard at all times if you are in politics. You may be in an elevator alone, minding your own business, when a young lady enters, talks to you briefly about the weather, and—when the elevator doors open on the main floor in front of many witnesses—slaps your face and starts screaming that you are a dirty old man. Just by coincidence, there are six cameramen there to record the event.

No candidate, politician, or elected official is safe. Whether you are running for dog catcher of Hooterville or president of the United States, there is a good chance your opponents will find a skeleton or create one (sorry Ms. Flowers) to make you look like a slimeball. The chance for a feminist to get a good payoff is excellent, especially if you don't want your campaign to end up in the toilet.

Looks like a 6 on this, but add a couple of points if you are running for president.

REAL ESTATE AGENTS

Because the sexual harassment suit against me and my companies was for many millions of dollars, you might think this is a high-risk profession. Not true. The frivolous suit was brought by a girl who worked in our office, not client. She was in a position to see tenants bringing in thousands of dollars in rent and deposits, and she logged them in and wrote receipts. She saw, felt, and smelled the money! I had a high profile in the community. But let's not dwell on my minor problem.

Real estate agents in general get into some of the same situations as appliance servicemen. There are not many jobs (excluding being a gigolo) where you get to take a lady into a bedroom—maybe even 15 different bedrooms in one day! In the real estate business you do this a lot, and many times it's just you and the client. If you are successful in negotiating a purchase offer or rental agreement for the client, you are probably safe. But if the client gets the hots for this shack and the owner or landlord passes her over for a better buyer or tenant, she may become the "lady scorned" and the sexual harassment game is there for her to play.

It is a good idea to take some other agent along when you are showing a unit. It's also nice if the other agent is of the opposite gender. Obviously if it takes two agents for every showing you are going to produce only half as much business, so if you don't smell trouble you may elect to go alone. In that case you may try a voice-actuated pocket tape recorder. One of my ace salespersons does it, and it certainly would prove valuable if a client ever files a suit or claim against him. Go to it, sell, rent, lease, show, and make the dollars you deserve.

This one only gets a 3.

LANDLORDS

My favorite occupation! Landlording was the subject of my first Paladin book (*Care and Feeding of Tenants*). When the sexual harassment charge against me and my companies became front page news, one of my ex-tenants

came forward with glee and contacted the attorney who was representing our accuser. This ex-tenant, who had resided in one of my apartments about three years earlier, claimed that I had also sexually harassed her. When she moved in she was an outpatient from a mental institution! She later had another tenant in the building arrested for rape! She claimed he raped her in his apartment. He was released on bail, and about a week later, she tried to have him arrested for rape again. Guess where she indicated the second rape took place . . . in his apartment! Now if a person were raped, would she go back for an encore the next week? She also accused her parish priest of rape and other misdeeds. Obviously this ex-tenant, whom I evicted, had problems that would render her a less than desirable witness against me.

Every landlord is a target for a disgruntled tenant. If you consider that every tenant has a grudge against his

landlord, and that that grudge gets bigger on the first of each month, you have a volatile situation. This disgruntled tenant can cause you problems at will by filing a sexual harassment complaint. If you expect to encounter trouble, it's best to take a couple of large witnesses with you to serve an eviction notice or confront a problem tenant.

Be careful, and don't give tenants a chance to grab your hard-earned money. This is a 4.

DISC JOCKEY

Now here is a "what if" for you. Being very conscious of what remarks or comments can be considered to be sexual harassing by feminazis, I listen to conversations and read articles very closely. When listening to radio and TV, I hear many hosts say objectionable things. Since they are not dealing one to one, as in a normal situation, they are actually harassing *hundreds of thousands* of thin-skinned ladies. What if these ladies took offense and filed a class-action sexual harassment suit? It's just a thought, but the way things are going I can see it happening. They file class-action suits against car manufacturers when the steering wheel comes off hundreds of similar models. (I hope I'm not giving the ambulance chasers any ideas.)

This one is impossible to score. I think this is a job for the Nielsen people!

FARMERS

We all depend on these guys for ham and eggs, some corn, our daily ration of veggies, etc. Could the following story ever appear in your local paper?

FARMER ACCUSED OF SEXUAL HARRASSMENT

Local agriculturist, Herb Horseball was accused of fondling a young lady. The event occured 12 years ago as Genny Gingham was helping her father deliver feed to the horseball tenant farm, out on route 99, just past the washed out bridge. Genny has indicated in her suite that Horseball "brushed up against her in a suggestive manner" as they were unloading her father's truck. She said the event traumatized her, she has not been able to sleep for the last 12 years, and that is why she filed the 32 million dollar suite. Her attorney, Mr. Shennagnas indicated he has an iron clad case and it is the best one of his career! Mr. Horseball is represented by the public defender, Abe Mouthpiece, Jr., and Abe says the claim is frivolous.

Herb Horseball has not been to town since the parade from the train station to the town square honoring our 3 boys who served in World War II. (Horseball was the one with the bandage on his head riding in the back of the undertaker's new Studebaker). Horseball received the Purple Heart (he has a plate in his head and must avoid microwave ovens) and has developed Alzheimer's disease. The trail will begin in March.

What's wrong with this story? The farmer is a tenant farmer. That means he has no property and probably no money! He is an introvert and hasn't been to town in 50 years. He's a nobody, with no money. He lacks any of the items the feminazis have on their checklist.

Let's test you on this one. You rate Herb. (If you gave him a minus 10, you're close.)

. . . .

I think you get the idea, so let's go over some others with less fanfare:

Cop	3	Factory worker	3
Fireman	2	Boss in factory	6
Bus driver	5	Grocery clerk	2
Cabbie	3	Truck driver	1
Bartender	1	Mailman	2
Lifeguard	7	Attorney	7
Pilot	1	Doctor	6
Carpenter	1	Dentist	5
Accountant	2	Priest	3
Janitor	1	Interior decorator	4
Mechanic	3	Barber/hairdresser	3
Artist	4	Undertaker	2
Boat captain	5	Jeweler	5
Builder	3	Photographer	4
Septic tank cleaner	0	Maytag serviceman	0
Yoga instructor	1	Caterer	1
Window washer	1.5	Insurance man	4
Mobster	0	Pimp	0
Lumberjack	1	Real estate appraiser	2
Marriage counselor	3	Garbage man	1
Hell's Angel	0	Restaurateur	4
Exterminator	1	Shoe salesman	1

Now here is how you kick the extra point. For every trait mentioned below that you possess, add the corresponding points to your score. If you get more than 15, you lose! More than 18, put the house in your wife's name and don't go out in public without your lawyer. More than 20, don't ever leave the house!

BONUS POINTS

Real well known, had your name or, even worse, your picture in the
local or national media in the last year   **2**
(It so happens that I had had my name on the front page 35 times in the
past 20 years and was on the cover of the local paper's Sunday magazine
section before I was hit with the lawsuit.)

In a position to hire, fire, promote, give raises   **1**
(That's me.)

Friendly, kind, considerate, polite   **2**
(That's me again.)

Prone to hug, embrace, console, or put your arm on or around someone
of the opposite sex while talking or assisting her   **3**
(Depends on what she looks like!)

Have lots of friends, clients, and customers of the opposite sex   **2**
(What else!)

Come in contact with more than 20 people per day   **2**
(If I didn't, I would be out of business.)

Occupation calls for one-on-one visits to homes on a daily basis   **3**
(Realtors make house calls!)

The name of your business and your last name are the same   **4**
(My company is Andy Kane Realty.)

Listed in Who's Who or on the lists of local or national "richest men in
the . . ."   **6**
(I am in *Who's Who in the East, Who's Who in Sales and Marketing, 5,000
Personalities of the World,* and a few more of these reference books.)

This is how the system works. Only in America can a sexual harassment suit be the reward for being successful. God bless America!

3. How to Avoid Becoming a Target

How can you avoid becoming a target? Boy, I wish I knew! You probably have watched a TV cop show or a flick at the local movie house where the cop collars a bad guy. The first thing he does, even before using his club or stun gun, is read him his rights. "You have the right to remain silent. Anything you say may be used against you. . ." You have probably heard it a thousand times. I'm going to change it a little, and I want you to cut it out and tape it to your bathroom mirror so you read it every day when you shave:

YOU HAVE THE RIGHT TO REMAIN SILENT... ANYTHING YOU SAY, DO OR THINK, MAY BE USED AGAINST YOU BY A FEMINAZI, FROM NOW UNTIL YOU DIE!

Avoiding sexual harassment charges is virtually impossible no matter what you do. I heard of an executive of a major company who entered an elevator. There were three women on the elevator and, being a friendly gentleman, well-known to the employees of the company, he said "Good morning, girls." Five years ago these women would have thought nothing of this remark and considered it polite, friendly, and even complimentary! Not so today. These feminazi-indoctrinated women filed a sexual harassment complaint because he had called adult females "girls." He didn't ask them to do the horizontal boogie. He didn't call them tramps, sluts, or whores. He just called them girls! Too bad he didn't have my warning taped to his mirror—it could have saved his company $30,000 bucks.

Avoiding sexual harassment is a very hard job. You have a better chance of getting hit by a sexual harassment suit than being hit by lightning. You can install a lightning rod on your building to ward off a lightning strike, but I don't know of any device you can screw on your head that will ward off a strike by the feminazis. I can, however, give you some things to watch out for:

1. *Females with hyphenated last names.* Mary Malone-Miginnis, Susan Neeley-Langford, etc. Usually when a woman gets married and insists on keeping her maiden name, it's so as not to appear subservient to her husband. But there may be other deep feelings that could result in animosity toward all males. Use caution when dealing with the hyphenated lady!

2. *"Users of Ms."* "Ms." before her name definitely shows a tendency to have strange feelings about her identity. She may take her insecurity out on you to prove how secure she is.

3. *Out-of-the-closet lesbians.* You may fear dealing with these ladies for fear they will charge you with harassment.

Amazingly enough, they are probably the safest to deal with, because the mere fact that they are out of the closet indicates they are self-confident and secure. If your actions or comments bother them, they will take care of it in their own way immediately (fist, slap, knee in the nuts, etc.). They will seldom take the cowardly course of filing sexual harassment charges.

4. *Women's organization members.* There are many organizations in every city that are for women only. Many occupations such as realtors, attorneys, doctors, or other professional occupations have their women's clubs. If a woman has self-confidence she will join a mainstream club, one that accepts males and females equally. Think about it. The goal of the women's movement is to have all women treated on equal footing with men, yet they form and join organizations that do not admit men! Confusing, but this seems to be accepted as politically correct.*

If you find yourself dealing with someone who belongs to a women's organization, use extreme caution. She has already demonstrated by joining the sob sisters club that she cannot relate to or get along with men, and she certainly lacks self-confidence. If she can find something in your attitude, speech, or appearance that she can claim is sexual harassment, she may file a suit to gain recognition and approval from her fellow sob sisters. If her charge garners enough publicity, she may even be elected the next grand potentate and exalted ruler of the Sacramento Sob Sisters!

Avoid women's organization members if you can. If you can't, take a witness or two, preferably female, with you when you must deal with them. Use extreme caution in any written communications too.

5. *Associates on the job.* Companies are so scared of being named in a sexual harassment suit that you have a

good chance of immediate dismissal for any allegation—not conviction, just an allegation! If you are a supervisor, your subordinate may resent your requests for a little more productivity in the widget factory. A sexual harassment complaint may be the way to get you off her back and out the door.

Don't give them the opportunity to railroad you. Meet with these people in open areas, not privately. Use group discussion to communicate, and if it is necessary to conduct a private meeting with a subordinate of the opposite sex, have another supervisor present. A tape recorder will also work wonders. Place the tape recorder in plain sight, and keep the tape in the subordinate's personnel file; just the thought of it will probably keep her from filing a frivolous charge.

If you plan to have witnesses present because you have concerns about a certain individual, select them wisely. They should *not* be close friends of the person you are dealing with; preferably they should be partial to you.

I recently ran into a case when a male meter reader doing his daily job came upon a female lifeguard at a community pool. He was polite, talked to her for about 10 minutes, and continued on his route. The lifeguard told her mother. The mother (not the lifeguard) filed a complaint with the power company, and the employee of six years was dismissed immediately. At a later hearing conducted by the state appeals board, the lifeguard and her mother failed to appear.

Did the judge dismiss the case and order the employee reinstated? Nope. Even though the accuser never appeared, the judge ruled that the power company was correct in dismissing the employee because of the allegations.

Companies often immediately dismiss someone who is only accused of sexual harassment, and the judges back

NEW YORK STATE UNEMPLOYMENT INSURANCE APPEAL BOARD
ADMINISTRATIVE LAW JUDGE SECTION

OPINION: Based upon the evidence at the hearing claimant was discharged following a customer's complaint of sexual harassment of a female employee while he was on a final warning. It has been held that sexual harassment is any unwanted sexual advance. By his own admission claimant delayed the performance of his job duties for over ten minutes to engage a customer's female employee in conversation. The undersigned cannot accept claimant's testimony that the conversation was ten minutes of banalities. His actions were clearly unwelcome. Claimant is subject to disqualification for misconduct in connection with the loss of his employment.

DECISION: The initial determination is sustained.

them up! If the employee had been accused of stealing and no evidence was presented at the appeal, do you think that the judge would have ruled in favor of the employee or the company? I am certain an employee accused of stealing would be reinstated immediately if not one shred of evidence could be presented to a court, but sexual harassment is a different ball game, with rules that even a major league umpire could not understand.

There are many other things to watch out for, but the main thing is to read the note on your mirror every morning!

You can also avoid sexual harassment suits by not becoming a sports star, politician, salesman, realtor, disc jockey, landlord, entertainer, etc. But every occupation has its risks and benefits. It's a risk just to walk out your door each morning, but if you don't you will be unable to avail yourself of all the benefits the good old USA has to offer.

The best way to avoid becoming a target is to minimize

your exposure by using caution. Let's take an example that may be familiar to you. Say you frequent a health club to keep your beautiful body in good working order. You walk in, and at one of the muscle machines you spot Sally, the receptionist at your office, working on a torture rack that she hopes will increase her bust measurements by 6 inches. Every female heads right to this machine when they arrive, and Sally is no exception. You have seen her there every day for the last month. You walk by, check out the increase in Sally's knockers, and offer a compliment. "Hi, Sally. Your chest looks great!" Just six little words. She smiles, says, "Oh Bob, you're a doll. Thanks a lot!" You then

proceed to the torture rack for the beer bellies and fat guys. She accepted your compliment and was happy that you noticed. She was still smiling an hour later when you left.

Now, turn the clock ahead about six hours. You are returning to the office after lunch. Sally is at her desk in her tight sweater. You pass by and say, "Hi, Sally. Your chest looks great." *Same six words* you used this morning at the health club that received the warm response from Sally, but this time she screams at the top of her large lungs, "You filthy pervert! You rotten scumbag! You dirty old man! I'm filing sexual harassment charges, and you will never work for this company again!"

You think back. "Didn't I say the same six words, in the same manner, to this same girl? Am I going nuts?"

It's hard to explain. If you had taken a gun and shot Sally to death that morning it would have been murder. If you took the same gun and killed her at noon, it still would have been murder. You used six words this morning and she liked it, and the same six words at noon cost your job, pension, dignity, standing in the community, and the coaching job with the little league.

The solution is you have to use extreme caution in speaking with anyone about anything that she could construe as sexual harassment.

Someone you trust and are friendly with today could easily turn on you tomorrow. If you are in business and pass over one person in favor of another, the passed-over chick may easily imagine that you sexually harassed her at lunch three years ago and bring up charges. There is no foolproof way to ensure that you won't be charged. The old, time-honored ways that were correct 10 or even 5 years ago in regard to treatment of females may not work today.

If your secretary or one of the girls in the shop comes in wearing snug jeans and you say, "Wow! Those jeans look great!" you have committed a no-no. The only comment you can legally use is, "You look good!" (or great, nice, fabulous, etc.). If your compliment is on a sweater, shirt, or jeans, you are calling attention to a *particular* body part, and this is not allowed. Your compliment must be general only. Also, be careful not to say, "You look good today," because this can be construed to mean that she did not look good yesterday!

Keep your ears open for words that could offend a feminazi. Absolutely do not use honey, sweetheart, darling, doll, or beautiful as salutations. A friend of mine in Florida recently related a story to me about these words. He said the owner of the lumberyard where he worked called all the employees in for a short meeting. The words honey, sweetheart, darling, and so forth were printed in large letters on the blackboard. He said, "Do you all know what these words mean?" And then he answered his own question: "Your job!" He then turned and walked out, short and sweet, but certainly to the point. That is a good example of how management feels about the danger of a sexual harassment suit.

Physical contact is possibly the worst violation that can occur. The pat on the rump or even on the shoulder can be considered harassment. I am aware of one incident in Buffalo, New York, where an employee touched a 68-year-old woman on the shoulder to get her attention because she was hard of hearing, and the touch cost that company a lot of money and created some bad publicity. You should try to keep a minimum of 6 inches between you and anyone you are dealing with. If you are prone to put your arm on someone or to touch her to emphasize a point, don't!

If you are in business, you also can be liable for what your employee or independent contractor does or says, even if he is out of the office as a salesperson and at some other location. It's a good idea to discuss the rules and codes of conduct with your employees on an ongoing basis, and be especially sure to include a chapter on sexual harassment in your employee handbook. I would suggest having all employees read and sign a copy of the handbook and keep it in their personal files.

Again, no matter how large or small your business is, you should have an employee manual that discusses sexual harassment. Written policies against sexual

Local Woman Awarded 150G In Sexual Harassment

NEW YORK — State Human Rights Commissioner Margarita Rosa has ruled that an employer is liable for the sexual harassment of an employee by a co-worker, even if that co-worker is an independent contractor, when the evidence shows that the employer was aware of the harassment but did not take effective steps to prevent it.

The order was issued in a case involving a Rochester woman who was harassed to the point of "stalking" by a salesman who worked for her employer.

Despite the fact she repeatedly apprised her supervisors of the man's behavior, they took no effective action, and she was forced to leave her job.

AS A RESULT of the violation of the State Human Rights Law the employer, Innovative Exteriors, Inc., 200 Buffalo Rd., Rochester, was ordered to pay Jacqueline Keltz $150,000 in compensatory damages, plus back pay with interest. The order marks a record amount in a sexual-harassment case brought before the Division of Human Rights.

Ms. Keltz has worked for the company as assistant to the telem- . . .

harassment are not required by law, but they may help prevent or limit such conduct and show management's commitment to ending it. Federal law specifically prohibits discrimination in employment on the basis of sex, and sexual harassment is recognized as one type of sexual discrimination. Sexual harassment in employment consists of "unwelcome sexual advances or requests for sexual favors and other verbal or physical conduct of a sexual nature."

There are two theories of sexual harassment. The first is when tangible job benefit or privilege is conditioned upon the employee's submission to sexual blackmail, and adverse consequences are threatened or implied if the employee refuses to cooperate. The "hostile environment" theory involves conduct that has the purpose or effect of unreasonably interfering with an individual's work performance or creating an intimidating, hostile, or offensive work environment.

I cannot emphasize it enough. If you own a business, you should have and enforce a policy against sexual discrimination. Those employers not doing so have been found liable for damages suffered by employees subjected to such discrimination.

The conduct of supervisors is particularly scrutinized by the courts, and employers may be held liable for their actions. Employers can argue that the supervisor was not acting within the scope of his employment when he sought sexual favors from a female employee, but it may be to no avail.

Employers can also be held liable for the creation of a hostile environment by a supervisor when the employer knew or had reason to know of the misconduct. The employer will be held liable for sexually harassing conduct when the employer is aware of the sexual harassment and fails to take reasonable steps to eliminate such offensive conduct.

The position of the Equal Employment Opportunity Commission (EEOC) is that the failure of an employer to establish a policy against sexual harassment and to deal effectively with specific complaints creates liability on the part of the employer based upon a theory of "apparent authority."

After the sexual harassment claim was made against our business, I prepared an employee manual with a section on sexual harassment, and I have reprinted it here. I am *not* an attorney, and I do not know if this will stand up to scrutiny by a court, but at least it addresses the subject and gives the court the impression that we are not condoning sexual harassment. If you have a small business, feel free to use any part of the section from our manual.

Be on guard at all times. It's a good idea to imagine that you are Indiana Jones and all women are poisonous snakes. Good luck!

> Federal law * provides that it shall be an unlawful discriminatory practice for any employer, because of the sex of a person, to terminate without just cause, to refuse to hire, or otherwise discriminate against that person with respect to any matter directly or indirectly related to employment. Harassment of an employee on the basis of sex violates this federal law.
>
> To help clarify what is unlawful sexual harassment, the federal Equal Employment Opportunity Commission has recently issued guidelines on the subject. Those guidelines state that unwelcome sexual advances, requests for sexual favors, and other verbal or physical conduct of a sexual nature will constitute unlawful sexual harassment when:
>
> 1. Submission to sexual conduct is an

explicit or inexplicit term or condition of an individual's employment.

2. The submission to or rejection of sexual conduct by an individual is the basis of an employment decision affecting that individual; or

3. When sexual advances, requests for sexual favors, or other verbal or physical conduct of a sexual nature have the purpose or effect of unreasonably interfering with an individual's work performance or creates an intimidating, hostile, or offensive working environment.

ANDY KANE REALTY DISAPPROVES OF ANY FORM OF SEXUAL HARASSMENT AT THE WORK-PLACE, INCLUDING ACTS OF NONEMPLOYEES. DISCIPLINARY ACTION WILL BE TAKEN PROMPTLY AGAINST ANY EMPLOYEE ENGAGING IN UNLAW-FUL SEXUAL HARASSMENT.

* Title VII of the Civil Rights Act of 1964.

FORMAL COMPLAINT PROCEDURE FOR SEXUAL HARASSMENT

1. Any employee who feels he or she has been the victim of sexual harassment should contact the management immediately. This report can be oral or written, but a written and signed statement of the complaint must be submitted by the complaining employee within three (3) days of the initial report so an investigation can proceed into the matter.

2. Upon the receipt of the written complaint, the management will contact the person who allegedly engaged in the sexual harassment and inform him or her of the basis of the complaint and the opportunity to respond.

3. Upon receipt of the response, the management will determine whether sexual harassment has occurred. Both parties will be notified of the decision.

4. If it is determined that sexual harassment has occurred, appropriate disciplinary action up to and including termination will be taken. The severity of the discipline will be determined by the severity and/or frequency of the offense.

5. An employee's failure to report the occurrence of sexual harassment within fourteen (14) days will be deemed a waiver of an intracompany action. Failure to file a written complaint within three (3) days of the initial report will be considered withdrawal of that report. If the person against whom the complaint of sexual harassment is filed fails to respond to the complaint within ten (10) days, the complaint will be taken as true and the appropriate disciplinary measure will be taken.

4. What to Do If You Are Charged

What should you do if you are hit with a sexual harassment suit? Find a really tall building with windows that open easily . . . just kidding. What you should do immediately is sit down in a nice quiet place and write down everything you remember about the incident. Include names of every person who was there, time, place, weather conditions, what was said by all people there, what everyone was wearing, and any situation previous to or after the encounter. Secure any calendars, written communications, notes, or articles that may be relevant in any way. If the accuser is or was an employee, make a list of any clients, customers, or other employees who may have come in contact with her. If the person bringing the charges did specific work, collect as much of her production as possible—good work, bad work, and rejected work.

Organize and keep all the information for your attorney and for your reference. After you have organized all the data, write up a complete history of your involvement so that you may give your attorney a written history for his use. Name names, cite dates, and list addresses so there is no confusion two years from now.

As your case becomes known to others, people will approach you with information as you run across them on a daily basis. Keep a small notebook with you at all times, and write down everything anyone tells you. Record dates and people's names and phone numbers. Keep this book by your bed at night. Many times I woke up from a sound sleep and remembered a person or event. If you go back to sleep without writing it down, you may never recall it again. You will be surprised at the things that occur to you at strange times. You'll remember things while you are driving down the road, sitting in a movie, having a drink at your favorite watering hole, or even while sitting on the throne. Keep that little book with you and write everything down.

I also would say don't keep your problems a secret, even though this is probably going to be contrary to what your attorney tells you. I would not divulge the exact circumstances to everyone you meet, because some may actually be friends of the accuser or spies for her attorney. But by discussing the general merits of the case, many people will remember events or circumstances involving the accuser, and this information may be very helpful in your defense.

All of the above information can be gathered before you pick your mouthpiece if your case is a civil and not a criminal matter. The big difference between a civil and criminal complaint is in the civil case you are served a summons and if you lose the case you can only lose money. In the case of a criminal complaint, the men in blue come for you with shiny bracelets. If you lose the case, you may pay with time *and* money!

If the charge is a criminal one, you should get an attorney immediately and talk to absolutely no one about your case or background. Luckily, most of the money grabbers go the civil and not the criminal route.

YOUR BACKGROUND

Since in defense of any harassment charge you will undoubtedly use events from your accuser's background to discredit her (arrests, dope use, alcoholism, previous complaints filed, bizarre acts, etc.), the attorney representing the accuser will be applying the same tactics to your past. Your attorney will need a complete history of your deeds or misdeeds. How far back is a good question, and the answer is as far as you can go. Start with your birth certificate. It should list a mother and father with the same last name for starters. Work up through schools, jobs, and hobbies, and list everything good or bad, *especially* the bad. Your attorney should not be surprised in court by information the opposing attorney introduces. If you tried to diddle the girl next to you in the third grade and Sister Theresa-Margaret caught you, your attorney can prepare a response (my client was enticed by her, he has since received counseling, etc.) And he will not look surprised in court.

My past is a bit unusual, and it took many pages to list my memorable events, but it had to be done. My hobby was auto racing, and in the day and age I was driving race cars (1950s-1960s), it was pretty rough and tumble. Various disputes were settled with jack handles and fists in the pits after a race. Being a red-blooded American boy, I was involved in a few decision-making melees. Racing today is a much better organized sport, and live TV reduces the chance of grudges being settled before the cameras, although it still does occur sometimes.

Many of my vacations are spent at clothes-optional resorts. I prefer these places because I hate to carry a big, heavy suitcase, wet bathing suits are uncomfortable, and I find the patrons of these establishments to be the most

friendly I have ever met. These resorts specialize in 24-hour fun! They are actually well run and closely supervised or there would be general havoc, but people who have never been to one may have a misconception as to what people do who are half-naked in the presence of the opposite sex (they do the same thing as people fully dressed do). Most of these resorts offer a brochure that explains their atmosphere. I got one and attached it to my dossier for my attorney's reference.

I have only been arrested for minor traffic and drinking offenses. Nothing obscene or immoral, just the things that most people do but don't get caught doing. I did it to a greater extent because I believe in living life to

its fullest, so my odds of getting a speeding ticket or two (or twenty) were higher. On one occasion about 20 years ago, I had an extra beer and got a driving-while-impaired violation that put me on a bicycle seat for 90 long days, but that's about it. I not only divulged these indiscretions to my attorney, I took it a step further (and you should do the same). I contacted the FBI via its Identification Division, Room 10104, Washington, D.C., 20537-9700,

enclosed a copy of my fingerprints made by the local police department, included a check for $17, and requested a copy of my record under the Freedom of Information Act. The document I received from the FBI was then given to my attorney for reference. This leaves no doubt as to your legal (or illegal) past and enables your attorney to prepare for any accusation that you have been arrested for some heinous crime in the past.

If your accuser has accused you of an act that took place at a specific place—office, home, car park, bar, etc.—photograph or videotape the location immediately. This is important, and it should be done by a third party who gives you an affidavit as to when and where the photos were taken. Many things can change in a specific location before the case hits the courtroom.

In my case, I had taken photos of the entire office for my records, but the opposing attorney, in a grandstand play to get publicity, actually went to the state Supreme Court to obtain an order allowing him to video my business office. We would have readily let him do this since most of the allegations were false ("naked women on calendars" was actually a tastefully done calendar from a plumbing company depicting 50 girls in bathing suits), but this attorney was very unreasonable, so we let him spend the time and money to bring the case to the court system.

My office has about 200 plaques, awards, degrees, and certificates on the walls. Three are awards to me from former presidents of the United States; one from Dan Quayle, our most famous vice president; and several from congressmen. There are two photos of me with topless girls. One is on a public beach and the other is at a clothing optional resort in Florida. The girls are topless only; I am dressed in jeans or a bathing suit. They are very tame pictures, and they are displayed in an area of my

Videotaping OKd in real estate office

By GREG LIVADAS
Times-Union

A state Supreme Court justice today allowed real estate agent Andy Kane's office to be videotaped after a former secretary claims she was sexually harassed while working for him.

Kane was said to have calendars depicting naked women on his walls.

, 22, claims Kane gave her a skimpy halter top to wear, with hand imprints on the front. He said he would pay her $1 extra a day to wear it, said her attorney,

, in court today to ask for the videotaping, held up the halter. He said the calendars would prove that the office was "a hostile work environment."

Justice Raymond Cornelius also agreed to allow   to amend her complaint. She had originally asked for $250,000 in damages. She is now able to sue Kane for up to $1 million — the limit established by Bankruptcy Court because Kane has filed for personal bankruptcy.

is also seeking $2 million in punitive damages.

A co-defendant in the lawsuit is Roy Forest, an employee of Allstate Rentals, another Kane business at 1942 E. Main St.

60

private office on a wall that cannot be seen, even by a casual visitor to the premises. If anything, I believe the video shows we run a highly respectable, professional office that has received numerous awards over the 25 years it has existed.

I have always had a limited budget for advertising. It is limited both by lack of funds and my reluctance to spend enormous sums when using unique methods to promote my company pays off better than extensive advertising. One of my methods is using unusual business cards. Twenty years ago, a friend of mine I will call "Bunny" was, for various reasons, working as a stripper. She worked area nightspots on a rotating basis, and she asked me how she could get the owner and patrons to remember her. I immediately said business cards! Since I always look for ways to advertise cheaply, I offered to produce her cards for her without cost if I could put my ad on the back. That way when she gave her card to a bar owner or patron, she also gave my ad out. I listed and sold several bars this way, and many of Bunny's patrons purchased homes or referred friends to me. This worked so well that I decided to make a few "special" cards to give to gentlemen I met at various events or taverns. I never mass-mailed or gave them to women, just individually to men where they were appropriate. I used only girls over 21 who signed releases. Since they were tastefully done and protected by the First Amendment, I felt they could not be used against me in the harassment case, but I made my attorney aware of them anyway.

Be sure to retrieve all the information from your attorney after the case is settled. Your attorney is sworn to confidentiality, but I'm sure his office is not Fort Knox. If your file should be stolen or borrowed by a disgruntled employee of the attorney or a burglar, you may be rendezvousing with someone under an overpass at 1 A.M. to present them with a suitcase full of money!

After the plaintiff's attorney was successful in leaking our plight to the paper, several articles appeared. The attorney for the person who accused us received calls from women who claimed that I had sexually harassed them in the past. There were four (I thought there would have been 400!), and they presented various ridiculous stories.

This is where keeping records is important. In checking through my files, I came up with files on three of the women. Two were ex-tenants whom I had to evict because of criminal or mental problems, and one was an ex-client whom I had purchased some property from, but the most interesting aspect was that all three of these women who had come forward had received letters from my attorney threatening legal action if they persisted in harassing me or my office staff.

The fourth woman was, I believe, someone who just wanted attention. Her story was completely fictitious, and she claimed that I had made sexual advances to her while I was hosting an open house on a specific street. She was unable to describe me to an investigator, I had never had a house listed on the street she named, and in fact I had had only one house open for inspection in the past 10 years, and that house was not in the town she mentioned! Some people like to get involved in prominent cases to gain attention for themselves. People even confess to murders they didn't commit in hope of getting some publicity! I guess they get tired of watching soap operas in the afternoon. Again, my records and that of the local real estate board proved I was not the person at the open house. My attorney received all the records on these women so that their testimony would not be a surprise and could be refuted immediately.

To work for you in a professional and proper manner, your attorney has to be fully informed. When someone keeps an event secret from his attorney, he is doing a disservice to himself that could easily result in his losing the case.

If, after you have presented your attorney with your dossier, you remember more events, be sure to get this information to your attorney. If you are not sure of the value of the photo from the company picnic, the credit card receipt for the massage, or the long-distance phone bill with the 1-900 sex numbers, give it to the attorney and let him decide.

Do not omit anything. I can't stress this enough. When you left out a few minor sins in your last confession, they will probably not surface again until you knock on the Pearly Gates, because J.C. does not employ sleazy private eyes like your accuser's attorney does. Unless your name is Genghis Khan, I am sure that your escapades will not be worse than mine!

5. Picking an Attorney

Possibly your most important decision in a sexual harassment case will be to select an attorney to represent you. I would not factor price into the process. I have found some expensive ones who are not worth it and delegate most of the pretrial work to an assistant who may be wet behind the ears. You pay for the number-one man in town and get number 999!

In some cases you will not get the opportunity to select your own attorney, such as when your insurance company accepts liability and provides your defense. It then has every right to select your attorney. If, however, the insurance company is providing a defense but has sent you a "letter of reservation," you are entitled to select your own attorney to be paid for by the insurance company. This letter of reservation technique is used when there is a question of liability on the part of the insurance carrier. The question would be, was the act in question *willful*? Did you grab the chick by the hooters and smile and drool? That's willful, and the insurance company definitely would not be liable for any judgment. Was the act *negligent*? Did you accidentally brush up against her hooters and continue about your business without any gratification or fanfare? That's not a willful act, and your carrier would most likely be obligated to pay a claim up to the amount of your liability coverage since your action was negligent but not willful.

The reason this letter of reservation is used is that sometimes the willful or negligent part cannot be determined until after the depositions and trial. It protects the insurance carrier, but it also lets you pick your own attorney, because if the company assigned you an attorney and you lost and it refused to cover the judgment, you could claim the attorney it picked was not up to par and did not provide an adequate defense.

92 ATTORNEYS

A

ATTORNEYS

continued

ATTENTION

There is no procedure in New York State for the certification of an attorney as a specialist except in the practice of admiralty, patent and trademark law. The Code of Professional Responsibility which governs the conduct of lawyers in this State, does, however, provide that "a lawyer or law firm may publicly identify one or more areas of the law in which the lawyer or law firm practices, or may state that the practice of lawyers or law firms is limited to one or more areas of law."

Monroe County
Bar Association

Now let's get back to a system for picking your mouthpiece. All your friends will recommend attorneys that they feel are great. They handled their house closing, their will, the adoption of their third world child; they are cheap; etc. But keep in mind who's on the railroad track. It's you, not them. Disregard their kind advice.

Should you let your fingers do the walking? The yellow pages are helpful, but let me illustrate one drawback. The size of the ad is designed to impress clients and attract business. The only requirement is that the advertisers *pay* for the spread. There is no requirement that you demonstrate proficiency in the field in which you claim to have superior expertise. It's just like Coke and Pepsi—each one tries to generate more sales of soda pop by bigger and better ads. Some publishers of telephone books even place a disclaimer or warning indicating that advertising by attorneys does not indicate that they excel in the classification but simply that they want to attract business in that category.

This is a good reason not to rely too heavily on the yellow pages (except for phone numbers and addresses). It's advertising, just like the "new and improved," "fat free," and "6 extra ounces" claims that you see in the supermarket ads. My attorney did not even have a

AREA   **HEINTZ—HELMEL 381**

..........467-9963   **HELLER Cheryl A** attorny
         73 State 14614 ....
         HELLER
         n 69 Parsils Ave 14609 ....

display ad in the yellow pages, just a one liner in plain type. That to me indicated confidence that she would be selected based upon her ability and not for flashing lights or hoopla.

If you have a personal attorney, he may know of an attorney who has expertise in this field. The local bar association may be able to recommend some who handle sexual harassment cases. One of the best methods is, of course, to find an attorney who has successfully defended a client on sexual harassment charges. Ask around, especially attorneys or people associated with the court system. Another source is court reporters. They usually follow particular stories and contact attorneys for additional information. You can also visit the newspaper section of the public library and scan the local papers for past articles on sexual harassment cases.

I have one suggestion. If you are a man being accused by a female, a jury will put more faith and credibility in your defense if it is presented by a lady lawyer. They will assume that this woman would not take the case of a defendant who has insulted or defiled one of her own species.

I would not take a bimbo lawyer just because she was a female. That would be counterproductive. You must find one who is smart and looks and acts like a female. If she is good looking, that will be a plus to the male jurors. If she appears to be gay (suit, tie, butch haircut, etc.), that may swing the jury away from your cause.

Once you have narrowed down your field to two or three, arrange for a personal interview with each one. Make notes of how easy it is to contact them and how fast they return your calls, and arrange a face-to-face visit. Ask if you will be dealing directly with him throughout the case (best) or with his paralegal. Ask what his feelings are regarding sexual harassment in general, if he had ever won a case of this nature, and anything else you want. Ask if he feels comfortable representing you, and ask yourself if you are comfortable with him.

Don't decide until you've looked at everyone you are considering. Sleep on it, review your observations, and then make a choice.

If you have some problem with the attorney after you get started, *do not* change attorneys. Work out the problem. It is very bad to change attorneys in midstream. No attorney can get the total picture from reading a transcript that your original attorney got from being present during actual examination of a witness or plaintiff.

Put all your faith and trust in the attorney you select, and you will have the best chance of winning the battle. Good luck in tipping the scales in your direction!

6. Insurance

If you deliberately harass some chick, you will probably not be entitled to any help from the "good hands people." Willful acts such as grabbing, using abusive language, forcing yourself on someone, or assault will be found to be outside the policy limits.

If you are the defendant in a sexual harassment case, you should immediately contact the insurance agent who produced your policy. If you are just a joe citizen and you don't own the company, or if you are only accused as an individual, your homeowner's or tenant's policy will come into play. If you are a business owner, then your business owner's liability policy will be activated.

If the person who accuses you claims she was physically or mentally harmed by your alleged actions and the alleged actions happened in a specific place (i.e., a building in which your office is located, a restaurant, etc.), and that location is clearly stated in the bill of particulars, you should also notify the insurance carrier for that location. If you own an office or business and all the alleged acts occurred there, you should also notify the carrier of your homeowner's or tenant's policy because if you are named as an individual *and* as the company president or officer in a suit, the insurance carrier that covers your company may not pay the portion of any award that applies to you as an individual.

All insurance companies have limits on when you must report any claim, and this is certainly fair to the company. If you neglect to report a claim, you may later be denied coverage. Obviously, it's best to report a claim as soon as you receive it. Make copies of the complaint, note the time and date you were served, compose a letter to state the basic facts, include your policy number, and send it to each company you feel may provide some or all of your coverage. "If in doubt, send it out." It's better to notify all than to miss one that may provide coverage. I indicated to include only the "basic facts" in the letter to the company. This is important, since until you are represented by an attorney and obtain his advice, you do not want to divulge any more information than possible. I would suggest a simple letter as follows:

```
                               JULY 10, 1994
WESCOTT INSURANCE
2675 DEWEY AVENUE
ROCHESTER, NY  14616
ATTN:  VIC WESCOTT

                    RE: BOP POLICY #AK007106
                        ██████ INSURANCE
MR. WESCOTT,
     ENCLOSED IS COPY OF SUMMONS AND COMPLAINT
SERVED ON ME PERSONALLY ON JULY 9TH AT 7:30 P.M.
THE COMPLAINTANT IS AN INDIVDUAL WHO WORKED AT
MY COMPANY AS AN INDEPENDENT CONTRACTOR FOR
SEVERAL WEEKS LAST YEAR.
     PLEASE FORWARD TO THE CARRIER.
                    THANK YOU,

                    ANDY KANE, PRES.
```

Send the letter registered mail, return receipt requested. Keep copies of all letters and correspondence from the company, the agent, or the attorney assigned by the company. Be sure to state in your letter how the summons was received by you (personal, mail, or tacked to your door), because different time periods usually apply, depending upon how you were served.

If your claim is accepted by the company, it will immediately assign an attorney to represent you. If its liability is clearly defined and it accepts the fact that if it loses the case, it loses the bucks, you are all set. If there is some question as to its liability and it issues a letter of reservation, you will probably need to select an attorney (see Chapter 5).

It's important to keep all documentation from the insurance company, especially letters denying coverage. Keep all insurance communication and a copy of your policy in one file for easy reference because you *will* need these items. Do not give the original policy to anyone; make copies and keep the original in a safe place.

If you are denied coverage or a defense, request exact reasons in wirting, question any individuals you talk to, and record their names and titles. Record times and dates too.

Your agent probably will not be able to determine if you have coverage because his basic training is in how to sell you a big policy on your house or offsprings so that he can reap big commissions and live happily ever after. He is not an attorney, so his legal knowledge may be limited. Insist that he record your claim and forward it to the carrier immediately. If the carrier has a local office and you are dealing directly with it and its people indicate that your coverage does not cover sexual harassment, insist that they obtain an opinion from the main office, clearly stating in writing the reason for the denial.

I was denied coverage three times along the line from agent to the main office, and each time I insisted on a review by a higher authority. Eventually I obtained an agreement to provide a defense with a letter of reservation. Do not give up.

If all attempts to secure coverage or a defense fails, you should obtain your own counsel—and his number-one priority will *not* be to defend you in the sexual harassment suit. Tell him you want him to review your policy and the company's denial of your claim immediately and make every effort to have the insurance carrier accept and defend your claim. You may want to even start a suit to obtain coverage from your insurance carrier. The reason for this is because a defense is costly and an award against you can be financially fatal. You and your attorney should do everything possible to obtain acceptance of your claim by the insurance carrier.

Dealing with insurance companies can be very hard and complicated. If you feel that you cannot handle the process, you may want to hire an attorney in the very beginning to submit your claim to the insurance carrier. Keep in mind that you have *paid* for coverage. You are not asking for charity. Your insurance company evaluated you as a risk, and it based your premium on that evaluation. You paid that premium without questions and relied on that company to cover you against all perils. You are not asking for anything for free; you paid for the insurance service, and you are entitled to it.

All states have insurance commissions or boards to regulate companies doing business in that state. These commissions have great power over companies. If there is a problem obtaining representation from your insurance carrier, ask *the carrier* for the phone number of the state commission. Just asking this one question may convince the pencil-necked geek at the insurance company that you mean business and are not going to roll over and play dead. If you don't get results from the company, call the state commission and file a complaint. One of the most important things you can do in the defense of a sexual harassment suit is to get the great financial and manpower resources of your insurance company behind your defense. An investigation process, deposition, and trial can cost hundreds of thousands of dollars!

7. More on Insurance

As I mentioned in the previous chapter, my insurance carrier denied me coverage, and I had to approach it three times to obtain a defense. Two years later, after providing hundreds of thousands of dollars for investigators and attorneys, the company began a lawsuit against us! The purpose of the suit was to determine the legal rights and responsibilities in respect to the policy.

What this indicated was that the insurance company did not know what the policy actually covered. If it could disclaim coverage by reciting a portion of the policy that excluded my claim, I would have received a letter that said, "You do not have coverage. See chapter II, paragraph 1c" or something like that. The fact that it brought the suit indicated that even the company could not understand its own policy!

Because the insurance company was providing all of our legal representation, those attorneys could not represent us against the company that had retained them. Therefore, we had to have our own attorneys represent us against the insurance carrier. Again, we had to go through the attorney-picking process. We filed a motion requesting to the defendants, Andy Kane Realty, Allstate Rentals, Roy Forrest and Andy Kane. Copies of the second reservation of rights letters are attached hereto as Exhibit "E".

8. Plaintiff seeks in this action a judicial determination of plaintiff's and defendants' rights under said insurance policy.

9. Plaintiff has no adequate remedy at law.

WHEREFORE, plaintiff demands judgment that this Court determine, construe and declare the legal rights and relations of the parties hereto with respect to said policy of insurance attached to this Complaint as Exhibit "A" and for other and

2

Exhibit A   Exhibit B   Exhibit C

the court to dismiss the suit and asked the court to award us attorneys' fees for this action.

One hot summer morning a few months later, we appeared in court accompanied by five high-priced attorneys. The court decided in our favor and dismissed the action brought by the insurance carrier. The court, however, did not award us attorneys' fees. Although we had to pay our attorneys, it certainly was a victory for us and well worth the money. (The court later issued an order to the insurance company to pay our attorneys, so we got our money back!)

Supreme Court Special Term

Monday, July 19,

Hon. Raymond E. Cornelius
Justice Presiding

9:30 A.M.

5—Aetna Life & Casualty Co v Andy Kane Realty et al — Martin & Labowitz — Dentino, Cammarata; John A Balluscio; Charles A Hall.

6—Thomas v Quigley et al — Wil- Osborn. Reed.

8. The Plaintiff's Attorney

As in any battle, each general tries to learn as much as possible about the opposing general. In any battle—and rest assured this case will be equal to a battle—the more you know about the opposing attorney, the better your chances of winning will be.

Attorneys who know the opposing attorney are a good resource, but because of their loyalty to their profession and fear of being sued for slander, they will probably not give you much information unless they know you well. Past clients of the opposing attorney are also an excellent source of information, especially if this attorney did *not* win their case. They may be able to tell you if the attorney buys testimony, creates evidence, lies, or uses investigators who are dishonest or break into homes and offices. (You say these techniques are only used in the movies? Don't bet on it!)

If the opposing attorney has won a case or two, they may have been covered in the daily paper. Go down and review the back issues and read any trial coverage you can find. You may even want to obtain a transcript of the trial.

If this attorney presently has a trial before an area judge, take a day off and attend, sitting inconspicuously in the gallery so as not to let the scum mouthpiece see you. Observe his techniques and what irritates him when questioning a witness. See how prepared he is. See how witnesses and the jury react to him. See what the verdict is.

Keep in mind that 50 percent of the attorneys practicing today graduated in the lower half of their class. Just because he has attorney after his name does not necessarily mean that he is smarter than you. You will pick up a lot of information through your observations and research.

If this attorney does anything that you feel is illegal or unethical, check it out. If you can document his over-stepping the law or the bar canons, you should bring it to the attention of the proper authorities immediately.

Every state has a bar that licenses attorneys and can suspend or revoke that license if facts warrent it. If you feel this attorney has broken any laws, check it out and file with the bar. Be sure to give any and all information you obtain to your attorney so that he can be better prepared also.

Any documents you receive from the plaintiff's attorney—subpoenas, summons, notices, etc.—should always be read by you and scrutinized carefully for errors. Save every document and have your attorney explain anything you do not understand. Many times you will discover a mistake that someone else would not because you are familiar with the names, dates, and places involved.

The opposing attorney has a lot to gain if he can win. A $1 million award against you will enrich his bank account by $333,333.33! I bet you can't even say that figure without taking a breath. Anyone with this much to gain may be inclined to take shortcuts, so keep your ears and eyes open for any activity by the opposing attorney that you may be able to use against him. That's the American way. God bless America!

9. The Bean Counter

While we are on the subject of attorneys and insurance companies, I think it's a good time to test your knowledge of what the most important factor is in determining the final outcome of your case.

Let's look at the factors in your case and see if you can determine the most important:

- ❏ Your attorney
- ❏ Her attorney
- ❏ Your reputation
- ❏ Her reputation
- ❏ The judge
- ❏ The jury
- ❏ The evidence
- ❏ Character witnesses
- ❏ The locale for the trial
- ❏ The bean counter
- ❏ Your appearance
- ❏ Her appearance
- ❏ Your guilt or innocence

Obviously all are important, but a little-known fact is going to come into play that hardly anyone thinks of . . .

the bean counter! That's number 1! If you checked the bean counter as being the most important factor, you are one smart cookie.

Every insurance company is in business to make money. To make money, it must not lose more money than it takes in on premiums. It does not care about your guilt or innocence; it does not care about your reputation. It just cares about making money, and really, that is the way it should be. If it paid every claim regardless of profit or loss, our policy premiums would skyrocket.

So here is where the bean counter comes in. After information on this claim is accumulated by investigation, depositions, adjusters, and attorneys, it is given to the bean counter. This guy is usually a beady-eyed, small-statured introvert. His office will be the size of a broom closet, and his name and title will not be on the door or in the main lobby directory downstairs.

Let's get into why this nerd is so important. In the past 10 years or so, because people did not know what to do with all the expensive computers they bought, they started keeping track of everything. I know people who live by the computer. They computerize everything: when to walk the dog, where he likes to poop, what time the paper arrives in the morning, how long a head of lettuce lasts in the refrigerator, their favorite recipe for chili, and numerous other unimportant facts. This way, they justify the king's ransom they paid for their personal computers.

The insurance industry and the legal profession have done quite the same thing, except that instead of where the dog likes to poop, they have entered the age, race, sex, and weight of jurors who returned a favorable verdict in a case such as yours. Where the date on the longevity of a head of lettuce is entered, the legal eagles have inserted the data on the size of a jury award for a case similar to yours.

Some statistics that the bean counter has access to include the time it takes for juries to decide awards and amounts based upon the locality of the trial (you may get a bigger award in one county where jurors are professional people used to dealing with big bucks, and less than half of that amount in an adjoining county where the jury pool is made up of farmers, retirees, and welfare recipients). The age, race, and sex of the jurors are also important. The judge may be critical. He has a lot of control over what a jury hears, and his past performance is noted for the bean counter.

The bean counter also factors in the cost of an investigation, hearings, motions, and other legal shenanigans, including a trial that could last several weeks or months, depending on the volume of evidence. All this data, including the bean counter's estimate of what the jury will award the little creep, is then factored into a big blender like your wife uses to prepare your porridge. He then will come out of his little cave like the groundhog does in the spring. (The main difference between Punxsutawney Phil and the bean counter is that Phil predicts how much longer winter will last based upon seeing his shadow, and the bean counter predicts the outcome of your case based upon the regurgitated data from his blender.)

One of the factors that does *not* enter into the bean counter's process is your innocence. The bean counter's decision will be based upon one thing, and that one thing is money. He will make his recommendation to the higher-ups to 1) offer to settle for x amount of dollars because a trial may cost $10x$ dollars, and a jury may award the creature $100,000x$ dollars, or 2) fight it out because it will probably go in your favor based on the local statistics, and even if the plaintiff wins a jury will only give her $1/2x$ dollars.

You will probably go through a lot of hearings and depositions before the bean counter's recommendation is applied to the case, and the reason for that is, again, money! Let's say it's early January and the insurance company has decided to offer x bucks to settle. The trial is on the calendar and will probably reach the court in late December. The insurance company will keep its decision and its offer secret from everyone until a day or so before it's ready to go to trial. Let's say, just for the hell of it, that the insurance company was going to offer a million bucks.

It probably has the million invested at 10 percent. That's a hundred grand a year in interest. By waiting from January to December, it reaped nearly $100,000 in interest. That's why you hear of so many cases being settled at the courtroom door. There is no reason for the insurance company to pay early.

While the insurance company is reaping its interest, you will be subject to ridicule, pressure, abuse from the press, and maybe even loss of income because you remain the alleged harasser.

You cannot talk to the bean counter because he is not available to talk to defendants. All his input is from discs, foldouts, graphs, charts, and other nonhuman sources. The insurance company may even deny the existence of the bean counter, but you have my word on it: he is there, and he will make the difference in your case!

10. Investigators

Your attorney or insurance carrier will hire an investigator to check out every fact or circumstance of the case. The investigator will check out your story in every detail, and he will check out the story of your accuser. While this is taking place, the attorney representing the accuser will also procure the assistance of an investigator to check out your background. He will be out to dig up any dirt he can on you, your associates, and your past mistakes and indiscretions. The plaintiff's investigator will have great incentive to smear you because it will endear him to the opposition, and he may even get a bonus for obtaining hard-to-get information. You never can tell what the plaintiff's investigator will do to acquire evidence or information.

You should warn your friends and neighbors to avoid contact with the plaintiff's investigator. Watch your rearview mirror for a tail. An investigator may follow you to establish a life-style or pattern (drinking, going to titty bars, picking up hookers, etc.). If you think you have a tail, try driving down a short, one-way street the wrong way when there is little traffic or exiting a drive-in restaurant through the entrance to the parking lot. If you have a tail, it will show up quickly. If you are sure you have a tail, go to St. Mary's and say a prayer, stop at an intersection and help an old lady across the street, and do some other nice things.

Did you ever hear that "one man's trash is another man's treasure"? Your trash can tell a lot about you, and any investigator, no matter how dumb, will take a peak at your trash. If you have any periodicals sent to your house other than the *Christian Science Monitor* or *Reader's Digest*, don't throw them away with your mailing label on them. If you read anything that a jury *might* find objectionable, rip off the mailing label and throw it in a Dumpster behind the 7-11. Look around your house. Do you have a gun book (you're a gun nut), a men's magazine (you're a

pervert), a rock magazine (you're a doper), and so on. Bills, credit card receipts, old checks, or bank statements may also be used to glean more information about you.

Throw every obstacle in the path of your accuser's investigator. Tell your friends that if they talk to the opponent's investigator, they will end up in depositions and maybe days of courtroom appearances (they may!), and they will lose much time and money in the deal.

Do you have a cordless phone in your house or a mobile phone in your car? These are dangerous things to use, not just because someone says you can get brain or ear cancer but because they transmit over the public airwaves. When something is sent in that manner, it is not illegal to listen in, so stay away from mobile or cordless phones at all times. Any investigator can park outside your shack and tune in to your conversations on a cordless phone. (The other person charged along with me talked to his daughter on a cordless phone from his palatial estate. The conversation was about the case, his previous marriage, and some other confidential matters. The very next day the opposing attorney had all the details of that conversation.) On the other hand, for an investigator to tap your phone line would require a court order, and it is doubtful a court would issue such an order in a civil case. When you use a hard-wired phone, you're pretty safe, but you still should use caution.

You remember the TV series and movie *The Fugitive*. Richard Kimball was always looking over his shoulder for Lieutenant Gerard. Keep looking over your shoulder for anyone who may be keeping an eye on your movements. It's better to be safe than sorry.

11. Depositions

What's a deposition? Good question. When a suit is filed, it does not go directly to a court, judge, and jury as you may have seen on TV. There is a "discovery" period, which may take several months or years.

A deposition is scheduled where both the accuser and the accused state their stories and are subject to questioning by the opposing attorneys. This is done under pretty much the same terms that an actual court case would be conducted, except that there is no judge or jury. The participants are sworn in, and all testimony is recorded by a court reporter. Witnesses are called, evidence presented and marked as exhibits, cross examination is heated, and objections are noted. This procedure is sometimes referred to as an EBT (examination before trial). Statements gained through this process will be used in the courtroom at the trial. If you or a witness say in the deposition that, "On August 11 at 3 P.M., I was standing at the corner of West and East Streets in the rain and I saw . . ." At the trial two years later, you say, "On August 11 at 3:30 P.M., I was standing at the corner of West and East Streets and I saw . . ." The opposing attorney will immediately pick up a transcript of your previous testimony and read it word for word. He will make an issue of your saying 3 P.M. before and 3:30 P.M. now. He will bring up the fact that you did not indicate it was raining. He will ask, "Are you lying now or were you lying then?" This will make you appear to the jury as a nincompoop, a liar, and basically a person who can't tell a story straight.

When you appear for a deposition, you should not go into details because they are hard to remember. The very best answer you can give to the opposing attorney is yes or no. Do not tell him anything you do not have too. If he asks a question that can be answered with a yes or no, answer yes or no and stop. The transcript of my testimony is full of pages of long questions from the opposing attorney and "yes," "no," or, "I don't know" from me.

Do not elaborate such as, "She was wearing a yellow dress, it was a Friday around noon, and it was the last week of July," because if you are not 100 percent correct, the opposing attorney may be able to prove that on that day she was wearing a gingham dress and was cleaning her uncle's barn!

Dress casual and comfortable. There is no jury to impress, and you should wear something that you feel comfortable in because you may be in a hot room for many hours.

I would recommend attending each and every deposition even if you are not required to. Your attorney may even suggest you do not attend. Disregard your attorney and be there anyway. You have a legal right to be at every proceeding involving your case. Why go? After all, you have a business to run, and you lose money when you take off work. But your reasons for attending are simple:

1. You know the true story. You will know every time a person bullshits the attorneys.

2. Unless you don't care about your case, you should hear and see everything that is to be presented to a jury.

3. Since most witnesses will tell phony stories behind your back, your mere presence will prevent some chicken-livered ones from lying. Sit there and stare at them from the moment they are sworn in until they leave.

4. By observing how witnesses dress, act, respond to attorney's questions, and other events of a deposition, you will get somewhat the effect a juror would get, and this helps you evaluate what areas of the case need more research and preparation. If someone appears good and is on the opposite side, you should spend time researching every statement they make so that they may be discredited later.

Your actions at a deposition should be well-planned. Keep in mind that attorneys and witnesses will be looking at you, your facial expressions, your body language, your writing on a pad, and your response when you hear detrimental comments from lying witnesses. These emotions can cause many things to happen. If a hostile witness is revealing important facts that may benefit your case and you suddenly look up, smile, jump with glee, or provide some other telltale sign, the witness will realize that his or her testimony is going to help you and may clam up. You should pick a comfortable position in your seat when not testifying and look at something in the room. Look out a window or at a painting, a light switch across the room, or some innocuous object like that. Stare at it and use this point for your gaze so that your expressions do not change as you hear testimony.

You may wish to write a message to your attorney regarding testimony that is being given. When an important issue comes up and you want to have your attorney ask questions or dig deeper, do not immediately write on your pad. It will be a giveaway to the opposing attorney as that you considered it important. Wait a few minutes and then write your note. You will have plenty of time.

It's also a good thing to get a copy of every deposition transcript and read it over. The pages and lines will all be marked. Keep track of the interesting items and reference them so you may find them later at the trial. Your attorney will also be doing this, but remember: you were there when the event supposedly took place, so you're more able to spot discrepancies, and two heads are better than one!

If this is your first experience in court, you will discover that most people will take an oath to "tell the truth, the whole truth, and nothing but the truth, so help me God" and then proceed to tell the biggest bunch of lies you ever heard. This may scare the hell out of you, but it's actually good for your case. The more lies they tell, the easier it will be for your attorney to show that they are fabricating their stories. This is also a good reason for *you* to stick to the truth.

12. The Media

Remember the note you have taped to your mirror: "You have the right to remain silent. Anything you say . . . etc."? This may be the best policy when it comes to dealing with the media. I say *may* because each person has his own circumstances to consider. Are you a private citizen who works for wages? If so, then it may be a good idea to keep your mouth shut. Just say "no comment" like the mass murderers and bank presidents who get caught with their hand in the till do. If you are a businessman and your reputation is on the line, I would highly suggest having a *prepared* statement to hand out without comment to the media. It must be carefully worded. An example is:

"We believe that this suit is entirely without merit and was filed by a disgruntled ex-employee who was dismissed for _____ (or "was passed over for promotion," etc.). Our investigation has uncovered not one fact to confirm any of the allegations, and we look forward to our day in court. Obviously if we conducted our business in the manner the claimant alleges, we would not have been in business for 25 years. If you desire additional information, please contact our attorney, Ms. _____ at 555-5555."

In my case, I have done many things to attract attention and free publicity to my business over the past quarter century. These things have placed my name and the name of my company before the public eye on hundreds of occasions. I have ridden a huge bull elephant from the Ringling Brothers and Barnum and Bailey Circus through the center of the city, raced automobiles, driven in demolition derbys at fairs, wrestled large dirty animals for charities, redesigned emergency vehicles to reduce accidents, made offers to purchase large arenas and housing projects slated for demolition, and ridden wild horses and bulls with *big* horns in rodeos. Each of these events graced the front page or made the 6 o'clock news because I cultivated the media. I cooperated in every way with their deadlines and tapings. I informed them of events in the real estate world that they may have missed, such as increases or decreases in mortgage rates or qualifications. By helping the media, I made many friends in the field, and when the news of the suit against my company was made public, I was immediately deluged by calls, visits, and requests for information and interviews by these same people. I deeply regretted the fact that I could not freely discuss the case and our defense, but I was limited to a simple statement such as the one I outlined above.

Most reporters do not want to hear your defense. It does not sell papers. Allegations, on the other hand, are always overblown. An allegation may include "severe permanent mental anguish," "future loss of earnings," or "permanent physical impairment," and using this will generate some good headlines for the paper, such as "Young girl severely injured by sexual harasser!" Needless to say, a jury may well decide that nothing happened and award her zero.

If you happen to have uncovered a skeleton or two in your accuser's past, you may want to anonymously forward a copy to someone in the media who is covering your case. I would forward *only* documents that could be acquired by anyone with access to public records—arrests for prostitution or drunken driving, credit reports, employment histories, complaints filed with government agencies, divorces, school records, or anything that reflects badly on the accuser's standing or reliability. If you have obtained anything illegally or under the table, I would not send that along.

Before you slip any information to the media, be sure its early revelation will not help your accuser. Many items are better left as surprises for the courtroom. If you divulge some dirty deed done by the scum who has accused you, it will give her attorney time to prepare a defense. If you spring it on her in court, her attorney will not be prepared.

When the trial is over and you win, take advantage of the situation and talk to the media. Rehearse what you plan to say and act professional. Don't say anything derogatory about the scum who put you through the wringer. Just make statements like:

"We knew from the beginning the courts would find us innocent."

"The facts were on our side."

"I thank the jury for their careful consideration of the facts."

"That poor girl should seek treatment."

If you own a business, invite the TV people to do the interview at your location. That way you get free publicity for your company, and it may counteract all the previous negative press. Nice country we live in. God bless America!

13. The Jury

The perfect jury would consist of 12 individuals who are your age, race, religion, height, weight, and nationality. They attended the same kindergarten, grade school, and high school as you. They are in the same trade, live in the same neighborhood, like the same TV shows and movies, and are married to 12 of your wife's sisters. These individuals would probably react and respond to all events in the same manner as you.

It would also be nice if we could have a thirteenth person just like you as the judge! But guess what . . . *it's not going to happen.* Since you will not be able to put your friends and family in the jury box, the next best thing is to select a jury who may like you or your style. You should be in on the selection of the jury regardless of what your attorney says. The reasons are simple. Your mere presence will indicate to the jurors that you care about the outcome of this case. I will also bet you that your accuser will not be there for jury selection because the less people this person has to face, the better she likes it.

The selection process is simple. The potential jurors are picked from a pool of registered voters, drivers, or property

owners in your area. They are sent into the courtroom one at a time and questioned about their beliefs and past experiences with situations like yours. Both attorneys will grill them. They have a certain number of jurors they can dismiss "without cause." That means they can shoot them down because they don't like their looks, sex, or anything else, and the attorney does not have to say why they were sent packing. The number of jurors that can be dismissed "for cause" is unlimited. For cause means that they have a past experience that would make their rendering an unbiased decision very remote. The past experience could be:

- Sexual harassment charges by or against them.
- Members of organizations that promote women's or men's rights.

- Friends of anyone involved, including the attorneys or judge.
- Past clients of the defendant, attorneys, accuser, etc.
- Relatives of anyone involved.
- People with predetermined opinions.

One more reason for you to be there during jury selection is that you may recognize someone whom you have dealt with in the past, and that person may not remember you (I had this happen once). If this does happen and you remember that the dealings were good (the horse came in and paid 100 to 1, the stock went out of sight, etc.), you may want to just ignore his lapse of memory and hope he remembers the pleasant experience after the trial moves along. If, however, your recollection is that the deal with the potential juror went sour (the horse dropped dead, the stock is now used as toilet paper, etc.), you should tell your attorney, pronto. Look each juror in the eye, keep the eye contact, and smile a lot. Let them know from the beginning that you are Mr. Nice Guy.

Where do jurors come from? Besides the previous qualifications, what turns an ordinary citizen into a juror? I believe the number one reason is boredom. You will notice that most jurors are retired, housewives, or people with blue collar jobs (taxi drivers, garbagemen, factory workers, etc.). Not that I'm trying to run these people down, because someone has to feed the pigeons, change diapers, and scare tourists from other countries. But I want to point out one amazing thing about our justice system. Did you ever hear of Donald Trump serving on a jury? Did the presidents of Xerox, Kodak, or General Motors ever serve on a jury? Why not? Because they find a way not to. They have a high-priced doctor pronounce them dead. Or they plead that if they take three weeks off from the conglomerate, it will fail and thousands of poor factory workers will hit the bricks. I know because I have been called and weaseled out of it myself. I must have done it 10 times because I do not want to sit in a courtroom and listen to someone's problems for five bucks a day when I can make $200 bucks a day solving my own problems.

This means that your jury will be made up of blue collar workers, retirees, and housewives who are tired of the soap operas. They look on this as a great opportunity to get dressed up, do something different, and be important for maybe the only time in their lives. They can eat in the courthouse cafeteria instead of brown bagging it. That's how our system works. You pick the best attorney who has 18 years of education, your opponent picks the best attorney she can find who also has 18 years of schooling, your case is assigned to a judge who probably was an attorney previously with 18 years of book learning and 10 or so more of real experience. That's a lot of education and knowledge! But do these professionals make the final decision on your innocence or guilt? Nope. Your fate is decided by a taxi driver, retired widget assembler, milkman, three bored housewives, stockboy, toll collector, parking lot attendant, house painter, plumber's helper, and grave digger!

That's how it works, so make the best of it. If you run into jurors—and you very well may since you will be at the same location, same parking lot, same elevator every day for some time—treat them cordially: "Hi." "Good morning." "Nice day." Do not discuss the case or offer them a bag of money. If you try to influence them in any way, you may hurt your case.

If the situation is such that it is not a direct contact, such as you are at one pay phone and a juror is next to you at another, you may try to plant a little seed or two. Face the phone like you did not recognize the cabbie or housewife and speak in a slightly higher tone than normal so your conversation gets overhead accidentally. Say something like, "I'm not sure the judge is going to let us bring up her prostitution arrests because they were two years ago," or, "We just discovered she has claimed sexual harassment at all of the last six places she worked," or, "We are trying to subpoena her lesbian girlfriends." Be sure not to acknowledge the juror at any time. This ploy also works in men's rooms when you believe a juror is in one of the stalls. Don't make it too obvious, but every little bit helps.

The jury system is about the best there is, but technically it's supposed to be a "jury of your peers." I take that to mean "people just like me." I doubt if they could find even one person like me. I am the president of a corporation, and I'm sure there will not be a president of a corporation on the jury. I am a retired race car driver, an avid naturist, a contractor, a published author, an environmental inspector, a licensed appraiser, and a licensed real estate broker. I have my own set of values, and although they may not be socially correct according to the latest fad, I feel very comfortable morally with them. There is absolutely no chance that another person like me exists in this universe.

Your attorney may have access to a data system or service that will help him pick the proper jury to hear your case. This information is based upon the makeup of hundreds of juries in the United States and what their decisions were based on in cases similar to yours. This is a good procedure, but it is not foolproof. I believe that innocence or guilt should be decided by a more scientific system than the one we have now. A possibility would be to have the jury evaluate each piece of evidence or testimony immediately after it's given. They could have a touchpad in front of them, and after each piece of evidence is presented, they could enter a score: +10 for believable and -10 for an out-and-out lie. Using these limits and the 20 digits in between for the maybes, a score could then be tabulated. The side with the highest score is the winner. Since this system is easily understood, however, it will never be adapted by the legal profession.

Best of luck with your jury.

14. Checking Out the *?#@% Who Filed the Charges

People who file false charges usually are not as pure as the driven snow. Anyone who would sacrifice their dignity, expose themselves to TV and press, and accept all the embarrassment that accompanies a sexual harassment charge just to reap a few pieces of silver probably has a pretty sordid past.

Your attorney and investigator will do their utmost to uncover any dirt on the plaintiff, but since your rear is on the chopping block, you should also do what you can to accumulate as much information as possible and relay it to your attorney.

Our case was what I certainly would call unusual, because the accuser had related many strange stories to us in the 11 weeks that she graced our office. Each and every story was a wingding. I will relate one here to give you an idea of her taste for the bizarre!

THE CAT STORY

One morning the plaintiff came into the office about 9 appearing very upset. She was on the verge of tears, and

later there were actual tears. She told me they had found her cat strangled with a noose around its neck hanging from the clothesline in her backyard. The cat had its stomach slit, and its guts were on the ground. They were sure it was someone familiar with the family because they had a large dog in the yard and it did not bark. The dog barked at all strangers. They had called the city and state police, and the police were watching the house at night and investigating the matter. She indicated that they thought it was part of a "Satanic ritual," and then she said to me that she had had a disagreement with another girl in our office and thought this girl had done this for revenge. She also said that the girl had been to her house and the dog was familiar with her.

She told and retold this story with great emotion to everyone who worked in or came to the office that entire day. But a strange thing happened the very next day. When she retold the story, she showed no emotion, just 24 hours after the tragic, horrible murder of her beloved cat! I made a mental note that she had certainly made a remarkable recovery from her sorrow and distress of the previous day. A few days later she announced with great fanfare that the culprits had been caught.

I had no idea that this story was not true. After the sexual harassment charges were filed against us, I immediately contacted the police departments that she said had investigated the cat sacrifice, and they had absolutely no report of anything like this. (I think they even thought I was the crazy one.) It was a hoax, a fabrication, and she had put one over on me and everyone she told the story to.

She had told the cat story to a *minimum* of 23 people in my office, not simultaneously but at least 23 separate times, once to each person, and those people all supplied us with signed affidavits that the cat story was indeed told to them by this girl.

As I mentioned, she was very convincing. I have had people try to put things over on me thousands of times, and I can count on one hand the number of people who succeeded. Yet this girl had me so convinced her cat had bit the dust, I nearly went out and bought her a kitten!

This story illustrates several important things:

• Even stories or facts told to you by a plaintiff that you perceived to be true may be out-and-out lies.

• You can do serious damage to a plaintiff's credibility if you can uncover stories or events like the cat story.

• Although I am not a psychiatrist, stories like this would indicate to me and possibly a jury that this person has some serious problems.

It appears that this story and many others that she created were simply imaginary events to call attention to herself. That's hardly something that a person with full deck would do!

A little checking on the plaintiff can produce some amazing results. If you know anyone who knows the plaintiff, ask them to find out what they can. This technique proved very valuable for me. After this girl came to work in my office, she recognized one of my clients as the father of an ex-girlfriend of hers. The "ex" is before girlfriend because the girl's parents had forbidden their daughter from ever associating with the plaintiff again because of a serious incident that resulted in hospitalization for his daughter and the plaintiff, plus a police investigation. I was able to obtain a copy of the police report from my client.

As I mentioned earlier, Roy and I are good old ass-kickers who do not quit easily. Roy has a habit of scanning the local legal paper daily. He looks at everything: judgments, divorces, deaths, disbarments, mortgages taken out or paid off, new corporations being formed, everything, including who is going belly up (bankruptcies) . . . and on Friday, April the twenty-fourth of 1992, lo and behold, Roy found that the plaintiff had declared bankruptcy.

Our accuser had filed a Chapter 7 bankruptcy. What was the importance in this little item? She listed her liabilities as $10,101 and her assets as $2,244. She did not, as required by federal law, divulge the multimillion dollar suit against us as an asset. This was fraud, plain and simple. She also went to great lengths to keep her attorney from finding out about her bankruptcy. The attorney who was handling the suit against us advertises himself in the yellow pages as an expert in bankruptcy, but she had used a different attorney to handle her federal bankruptcy filing! She was hoping no one would discover the Chapter 7 filing, but old eagle-eye Roy does not let much get past him.

Now why did we get excited over a bankruptcy? When a bankruptcy filing becomes public knowledge, you can obtain a copy. That copy lists all of the person's creditors, and you will be amazed at what you can tell about a person by looking at a list of her creditors. Our accuser had indicated that she was in good condition physically before she came to work for us, but we caused her to get an ulcer! Yet her bankruptcy indicated *seven* trips to the hospital. That's a lot of hospital visits for a person in good condition! Since she had to swear to the accuracy of her petition, it also showed her disregard for the truth since she neglected to include the multimillion dollar suit against us. (It was later amended to include the suit.)

Ask anyone you know who lives near your accuser, works with her, or has any contact with her or her family to keep you informed of any events, even seemingly insignificant ones. You will find out a lot of information in this manner. For example, a member of our accuser's parish supplied us with a Sunday bulletin indicating that our accuser would be married shortly. This was important to us because the girl had claimed the trauma of working in my office had created a "fear of men" that made her unable "to form relationships with members of the opposite sex." Her marriage, even though the person who sent us the bulletin from the church thought little of it, was actually a blessed event for us because it disproved one of her allegations!

Dig, dig, dig! You will be surprised at what you will find out. Since you will most likely know your accuser better than your attorney or his investigator will, there is a good chance you will turn something up. Do not do anything illegal, such as breaking and entering, or you could damage your own credibility. A bribe here and there or a quart or two of scotch will usually get you just about anything you want. Documents are better than hearsay, and photos or videotapes are excellent. You should think back over any circumstances that could have generated photos (retirement parties, company picnics, office photos, etc.). We were able to find various photos of our accuser, dressed in brief attire, hugging older gentlemen at a company retirement party.

Dig, dig, dig! There is gold in the accuser's background.

15. Witnesses

Because you will probably furnish the names of the witnesses to your attorney and investigator, you obviously are in a good position to give them additional information. It's best to do it in writing so they can refer to it later, and if you do it verbally some details may be forgotten.

Here's an example of the data I provided on one witness: "Very mature for her age, has child from previous marriage, presently living with computer programmer, has owned her own home but presently residing in boyfriend's house, has college degree in teaching field, always dresses professionally, drinks occasionally (wine/beer only; no hard liquor), worked as teacher before coming to our company, had lunch with accuser on several occasions, went dancing with accuser and boyfriend, etc."

Put everything in a short statement and give it to your attorney. Keep one copy for yourself and add to it as things come up. I would suggest "refreshing" witnesses' memories by giving them other witnesses' statements to read or telling them what others said, but *never, never* suggest that they outright lie or embellish the truth. A lie can come back to haunt you and may make everything else that witness says unbelievable. Believe it or not, the truth is the answer. (Do I sound like a Southern preacher?)

I'm not saying that you should encourage a witness to describe every detail truthfully, because some items may be better left unsaid. If you or your attorney thinks a witness will hurt your cause by telling the truth, just eliminate that witness and hope the other side does not call him.

This happened to me. I had a very good, honest witness who had socialized with our accuser on various occasions (i.e., picked up guys with her) and was aware of many of her deeds. She would have been one of the best possible witnesses for me, but she had had a slight marital problem at one time *and stabbed her husband!* It was just one of those deals, and in her native country, a woman stabbing her husband was not a big thing, since the women of that country are known to be excitable. If we had used this lovely girl, the opposing attorney would certainly have made a big deal out of the marital conflict and discredited her and us.

Some of your present friends may volunteer to become witnesses, even though they knew nothing about the case. (I had many!) Thank them and politely pass on their offer. The best witnesses are people who are *not* your friends or associates. A jury will look with a jaundiced eye on close friends of yours. The ones who carry the most weight will be people who have come in contact with you or your accuser through business or at social functions or other casual or one-time occasions because they are removed from your influence or the scuttlebutt of your environment. If witnesses are employees or friends of yours, however, be careful not to alienate or fire them before the conclusion of your case.

In our case, the accuser had many occasions, when acting as a receptionist, to deal with clients off the street who had never even met me. Because most of our work revolves around documentation (leases, purchase offers, etc.), I was able to reconstruct events during the time of her employment and contact many potential witnesses. Interviews are more valuable if they are done by your attorney or his investigator. You should avoid talking about the case with the witness until statements have been taken by a third party so as not to influence the witness.

My comment to each and every witness who asked my advise was the same: *tell the truth*. It worked well for us, and it will for you.

24. Offer to Settle

After both sides have had an opportunity to examine (take statements under oath) everybody and evaluate the strength of their case, there *may* be an offer by one side or the other to settle the action. Either side can make the offer, and it is negotiated just like any deal. One side may offer to settle for a 100 grand, the other comes back with 75 grand, and later a figure of $82,511.39 is agreed upon by both. You will have very little input into this proceeding (unless you do not have any type of insurance; then it is wise to be involved since it's your bucks), and it is based upon many factors as determined by the bean counter. Some of the factors are:

- Cost of trial in terms of manpower
- Possible amount awarded by jury
- Odds of jury going against you
- Venue of the case (big awards in big city, small awards in Hicksville)

The offer to settle in no way affects the amount asked of or awarded by a jury if a trail occurs later, as it is not admissible. You can't say, "This person wants $10 million in her claim, but last month she offered to settle for a thousand bucks!" The settlement offer is nothing more than an out for both sides to avoid the time and expense of a trial. It may work and it may not, and each case is judged by its merits. I can't advise you to go for it or dig your heels in. You have to decide this deal on your gut feeling, based, of course, on the strength of your case.

Many times you can add a confidentiality clause to an offer that prevents either side from releasing the settlement figure to the press or divulging it in any way. This will prevent another person from knowing that you will pay x amount of bucks to avoid being dragged through a trial and pulling a trick similar to this scam.

Settlement offers do not come early in the proceedings because each side has to feel out the other and weigh the evidence. If an insurance company is involved, it is to its advantage to stall as long as possible because it is collecting interest on its money, and for this reason you hear of many cases being settled "at the courtroom door." They held onto their bucks till the last second. A few years ago I was involved in a personal injury case, and the insurance company waited until the case was heard and the jury had started to deliberate to offer me a settlement. (I took it!) That's definitely brinkmanship.

Consult your attorney, rely on your gut feelings, and disregard the automatic response of "I didn't do it so why should I pay!" Money is money. If you can get rid of the problem by shelling out a peck of cash, you may be saving bushels of bucks that a jury may otherwise award to your accuser.

17. The Trial

Although nothing will probably ever be as spectacular as the O.J. Simpson trial for media coverage (the judge in that case even received letters from Tibet!), there is a good chance the press will stick their nose into your problems because the word "sex" sells fish wrappers and attracts viewers to the 11 o'clock news.

By this time you have had a dry run with your attorney and have discussed the merits of the case. Let's consider some items:

YOUR ATTITUDE

The best attitude is "I know there is a problem here; I'm just here to straighten it out." Do not act or appear defensive.

NERVOUSNESS

This is common. Every person will be nervous in this situation. Even the Pope is nervous before he walks out on the balcony to address 100,000 people. Rock stars who perform 300 nights a year are nervous before they hit the stage, but once they are on the balcony or in the spotlight, this nervousness disappears.

I have had this same feeling hundreds of times. I do radio shows promoting my books. There is absolutely no way to prepare for a show when it is impossible to predict what the next caller may say. All of my shows are live, with no 10-second delay. You can't make a mistake.

I used to get very nervous waiting for a show to start. I solved this problem by finding something to do such as reading a book instead of just sitting there shaking. When I raced cars, the period of time between driver intro-duction and "gentlemen start your engines" was more terrifying than when the green flag flew and we were dueling, wheel to wheel, at breakneck speed and our lives were actually in danger. Every driver told me he felt the same way. Most drivers pass this nervous time by doing something—wiping off the car, cleaning their goggles for the tenth time, checking tire pressure, or performing some other menial task to keep their mind busy. I assure you, once this deal gets under way, nervousness will disappear!

DRESS

The jury will be made up of people of limited means. They will be wearing their Sunday best (or funeral or wedding attire). Their threads will not be tailor made. They will be wearing off-the-rack clothes from K-Mart, J.C. Penney, and Sears. If you show up in a silk suit that cost more than the second-hand car the juror drove to court, he or she will take a disliking to you immediately. You should be neat, have a haircut to accommodate your age, and wear a stylish suit with a conservative tie and white shirt. I would *not* wear a black or dark blue suit because this seems to be the costume lawyers prefer. Lawyers are not the most likable species in America, and you certainly don't want to be identified with them in the jurors' mind. Be sure to have several suits or combinations to wear, and wear the best one the first time you come in contact with the jury, even if that is during jury selection. Shoes are preferable to boots, unless you live in the West where boots are the norm.

JEWELRY

A no-no. No gold pins, chains, or bracelets. A wedding ring is OK if you are married. So's a conservative watch, not a diamond-studded razzle-dazzle deal that blinds the jury every time you check to see if it's lunchtime. A lapel pin is OK for a realtor, mason, or other organization member as long as there is no chance it will offend one of the jurors.

GLASSES

If you *must* wear glasses in court, be sure that your eyes are visible. No photogray, sunglasses, or thick glasses. If you have thick or bifocal specs, meet with your optometrist and get contacts or special glasses without bifocals just for the trial. Any time you do not need the glasses, take them off so the jury can see your eyes.

POSTURE

During this entire trial the jury is going to be looking at you. No matter what earth-shaking revelation that the current witness is revealing on the stand, the jury is going to be looking at *you*. They want to see how you react. They are analyzing you at *all* times. Never let your guard down. Don't pick your nose, ear, or ass. Don't slouch in your chair. Don't ogle any females no matter how good looking they are, how high their heels are, or how short their skirts are. After you beat this deal, you can indulge your mind at the closest Hooters emporium.

Take notes, pay attention, don't daydream. Look sharp all the time!

FOOD/DRINK

Avoid consuming large amounts of either. This cuts down on trips to the head. You do not want to miss one minute because if you go out during the trial, a vital bit of testimony may be heard and you might be the only one that can warn your attorney that the testimony is false.

If you are going to be on the stand, absolutely do not drink or eat anything more than is enough to keep you alive. It's hard to concentrate when your bladder is about to rupture. As you testify, you will see a nice big glass of ice water at your fingertips. *Do not* drink this water. If your mouth is dry, just take a sip and wet your whistle. If you gulp this stuff, you will be very uncomfortable in five minutes.

ANSWERS

Review your deposition the night before. No one is perfect, and if you make an error, do not get excited, even when the opposing attorney makes an issue of it. The jury knows that these events took place two or three years ago, and a slip once or twice is unavoidable.

Just answer the question. Do not volunteer any extra unless your attorney is trying to bring out a particular aspect and is leading you in that direction. *Do not lie.*

FAMILY

If you are a family man, having your wife and an adult kid or two in the courtroom will not hurt your case. They should not be dressed to the nines, though; their funeral clothes will do. If your wife says that this lawsuit is your problem and she does not have the time to go to court, you may mention that if a verdict exceeds your coverage, the family may be living in a large tent in a public park instead of the nice, cozy home you now enjoy. She should see the light!

One word of warning regarding your wife: if you are in your fifties and your wife and the girl who is accusing you appear to be or are actually in their twenties, do not bring your wife to court. The jury could surmise that you have an appetite for cute young things and turn against you. One solution to the beauty queen wife problem is to borrow a friend's matronly wife, leave your bleached blonde wife home, and arrive daily with the impostor. Do not introduce her to anyone as your wife; just bring her with you and the jury will assume that she is your wife.

OUTSIDE THE COURT

Be careful during breaks, lunch, and before and after court, because the jurors have the same habits you do. They eat, drink, drive, and go to the bathroom. You may be in close proximity to the jurors without knowing it, and they will be observing you even though it is not in the courtroom. You must make a good impression at all times, not just inside the courtroom. Never discuss your case in the bathroom; you never know who's in the stalls. I also would avoid smoking anywhere you can be seen. Many people today have come to believe that those who smoke are morally inferior based upon the negative impact that the health people have created. You don't want to create *any* adverse impressions.

EYE TO EYE

The jury likes to have answers addressed to them. It makes them feel important. When answering, look at the attorney who is grilling you and the jury alternately. I usually look at every juror for a few seconds each so they each feel included.

. . . .

All in all, you probably will not have any surprises during your trial. Perry Mason and Ben Matlock are strictly TV productions, and it's very doubtful that any surprise witnesses will appear. The attorneys are required to submit the names of witnesses they will call and evidence they will present previous to the trial. There is little chance that the topless dancer you befriended in 1963 will show up as a witness.

Keep cool, don't show emotion, and don't look at the ceiling and roll your eyes when you hear lies being told about you. Stay alert at all times and quietly indicate to your attorney any items that appear out of line. Do this verbally or by writing notes.

If you have a good judge and jury, and if you are really blameless, you will possibly win.

18. Preservation of Assets

If you have just been named in a sexual harassment suit, it's probably too late to protect any assets that you already have. Property transfers could be reversed at a later date by a court if they were done to deprive a potential creditor. Check with your attorney. I would also consult with an attorney who specializes in bankruptcy. Many judgments obtained through a sexual harassment suit can be discharged through a bankruptcy filing. That's about it for your assets *as of the time you are sued*, but from the time you are served until trial can take several years! Do not—I emphasize, *do not*—add to your portfolio any more assets that the accuser may grab in the event of an award that exceeds your coverage. If you are going to buy a new house/car/boat or other big-ticket item and you are placing a big down payment, that equity could be attached and sold with the proceeds going to your adversary. You would be wiser to keep your assets stationary.

If you *must* have a new yacht during this time, it may be smart to buy it in your wife's or child's name. You could also form a corporation for investing during this period of time. If everything works out OK and you are home free, you can always transfer these new toys back to your name. You should definitely seek advice from an attorney and/or accountant during this period.

Remember, anything you add to your portfolio may be taken by your opponent if she wins. This applies to lottery winnings or any other game of chance that might pay off big, so plan ahead. When you plunk down your buck for a ticket of chance, use your wife's or your corporation's name just in case you are a winner.

The same idea applies if you are a business owner. New equipment or property could be taken if an award exceeds your coverage. Lease instead of buy, or buy using a new corporation and lease back to your present business.

Any large sums of money should be placed in an account other than yours. If Aunt Minnie dies and leaves you a few grand, place it in your wife's grocery account, not your checking account.

You may be 100 percent sure you are going to win your case, but it's foolish to take any chances.

19. Ozzie and Harriet Are Dead

In the early years of the tube, the top-rated show was about a family. It was called *Ozzie and Harriet*. Even stranger was the fact that the four actors who played in this early sitcom were indeed a real family. The youths of that period identified with the two boys in the show. If David or Ricky restyled their hair, the youths of that time headed for the barbershops. If David or Ricky wore a cardigan, cardigans immediately became the rage. This family mirrored a large portion of the families in the United States. Ozzie went to work each day. Harriet put an apron on and stayed home, cooking and caring for the two kids.

To show you how much our society has changed in the past decade or so, let me illustrate how this family would be perceived today.

As I mentioned previously, I sell real estate. If Ozzie and Harriet were alive today and I sold them a home, it might be good advertising to take their photo in front of their new home. If I put this photo of the most all-American, wholesome, conventional family in the world in the local paper and indicated that I had just sold them a home in the Berry Bush subdivision, I would *immediately lose my license to*

sell real estate! How could this be? The main reason is this family is all white! The law says that I could be indicating that this subdivision is for whites only. The only photo I could use would have to show the racial makeup of the families in the area. If the neighborhood was 25 percent white, 25 percent African-American, 25 percent Asian, and 25 percent Latino, I could show a white guy with an African-American lady, a Chinese kid, and a Mexican kid in front of this house. If a French poodle got into the photo, I would probably have to find a German shepherd to balance off the pose! These crazy rules, along with hundreds of others, have crept into our society without much fanfare. Some are logical, some are not, but all have to be adhered to. There is even a rule that says if I offer a hillside home with a panoramic view of 10,000 surrounding acres of forests, waterfalls, and mountains, I cannot say in the ad "spectacular view" because it could be offensive to a blind person! (How could the blind person read the ad?) I cannot say "bachelor pad" because it is sexist. I cannot offer a "handyman special" for the same reason. I also cannot turn down a drug addict as a tenant because drug addiction is considered a disability under federal law, and I am not allowed to discriminate against the disabled. The maximum fine for breaking these laws is $50,000.

This just gives you an idea of what the do-gooders and feminists have done to our country. The sexual harassment guidelines are so vague, and the fact that the supposed victim is allowed to determine what they think is offensive, is completely ridiculous. Any good-natured comment that would have been graciously accepted during the Ozzie and Harriet era can now lead to lawsuits, disgrace, loss of job, and poverty!

In the Ozzie and Harriet era, people behaved nicely to each other. People extended courtesies to older people. Men opened doors for women and gave up their seats on the bus for someone who needed it. These rules were very informal, and they were the result of good upbringing by caring parents. Now, that informal mandate for public behavior has been replaced by more formal rules and government-based laws. The question "Is it proper?" has been replaced by "Is it legal?" Many people are actually afraid to practice good manners because they may be sued for treating a woman differently than they would a man.

Is our world better off with all the absurd rules and regulations instigated by feminazis and do-gooders? You decide!

Conclusion

The world is changing. Laws are enacted with little fanfare that can make the everyday actions of you and your friends illegal! Your reputation and your money are at stake. The ambulance chasers have a whole new field to cultivate, and it's lucrative, so they will be filing suits in greater and greater numbers. You must begin using caution immediately. Evangelist preacher Billy Graham, a likely target because of his bucks and reputation, refuses to ride alone with any woman (except his wife) in a vehicle. If this saintly gentleman is this cautious, shouldn't you be?

If you are an employer, you should discuss sexual harassment with your employees. I firmly believe that certain females go from place to place looking for a situation to file a suit over. You should make your employees aware that the cute young thing coming on to them may really be setting them up for a lawsuit and not a trip to the sack.

Look around your shop or factory to see if anything objectionable is in sight. A mechanic's calendar pasted to his toolbox is enough to cause problems if a customer or other employee does not like it. Even an innocent pinup calendar of a fully clothed chick can get you into problems. The calendar on our wall that the greedy girl claimed was objectionable was issued by one of the largest corporations in America, and it had issued *hundreds of thousands* for 40 years without complaints. Check out your premises on a regular basis. Someone may put up an objectionable item five minutes after you do your walk-through.

You are liable for what your employees do, and, incidentally, independent contractors who work indirectly for you may still be considered an employee if a suit is filed because they work under your direction. Even employees or friends of many years may turn against you if they think they can reap a big enough cash reward. It's like winning the lottery, and they don't even have to buy a ticket!

If you are in public office, you must be especially careful because the party that wants your job is looking at all your moves. They will be talking to your staff and volunteers just looking for an indiscretion. Bill Clinton and his sexual harassment problem is a good example.

As I mentioned previously, if you are well known or in any way popular in your area, you are a target. You must use caution in all your dealings. The chances of being charged in criminal court are remote unless the charges are filed to enhance a later civil suit. Most plaintiffs are looking for money, and that is only possible in civil courts.

Any charge that has the word sexual in it will attract media attention. Be careful when dealing with the media. If you are approached by the media, stop and reread Chapter 12.

You may think it could never happen to you. I did. I always felt that my employees and I were dealing with the opposite sex in an appropriate manner, and I even have hundreds of letters from satisfied customers to back up my observations, but it only takes one person looking for a big score to throw a monkey wrench into the works.

Warn your family that someone may try to get at your money by using one of them as a target. Your wife or kids may be entrapped by a gold digger and file a suit, hoping you will step in and bankroll a settlement to protect your family name.

People don't use electrical appliances during lightning storms, and that's good. But your chances of being hit by a sexual harassment suit are better than being hit by lightning! *Use caution around the opposite sex!*

Our Case:
The Final Chapter

In our case, after 3 1/2 years of depositions, hearings, transcripts, investigations, and meetings, an out-of-court settlement was reached. A release was signed, and this horrible event was put to rest.

If you encounter a suit and offer to settle, be sure the offer meets other criteria besides the monetary considerations. If you are a businessman, you should include a provision to eliminate the possibility of adverse publicity. You should also insist on a clause that indicates the settlement was reached to avoid the cost, time, and nuisance of a trial, and that there is *no admission of guilt*.

I was both happy and sad that we had reached an agreement. I was happy because 1) I could plan vacations without wondering if I might lose my downstroke or a trial would coincide with my trip; 2) the very good people who came to our aid would now not be required to appear in court; 3) my business would not be jeopardized by adverse publicity or an award against us, hurting not only me but the wonderful people who make up our companies; and 4) I did not have to be in the same room with the plaintiff or her attorney ever again. I was sad because I believe a trial would have completely vindicated us!

I was always amazed at the press coverage our case generated. By actual measurement, it consumed 29 column inches in the local papers, plus assorted major TV and radio exposure. When President Clinton was accused of sexual harassment, his story in the same publications totaled only 7 column inches.

Another interesting aspect of this case was the attorneys' efforts to settle it. I'm a businessman; I like money. If the case were to be tried, the carrier and others involved estimated that it would take up to three weeks! When on trial, attorneys put in long days—15 or 20 hours a day is not uncommon. Now if I was assured 3 weeks of 15-hour days at gigantic hourly rates, why would I want to see a settlement? The attorneys each could have bought a new Cadillac and had enough left over for a tropical vacation! Since I was curious as to why they would heartily and vigorously attack the opportunity to upgrade their wheels and soak up some sun and rum, I asked these puzzling questions. Their answer: attorneys are supposed to do what is best for their clients, not themselves. Since we were being represented by the local "dream team" of legal minds, they were doing their utmost to consider our best interests, and the Cadillac and trips were not a factor in the efforts of these superb attorneys. That sure as hell shoots holes in the lawyer jokes!

While we are on the subject of attorneys, I have to relate a couple of experiences that occurred with our two main lawyers. Keep in mind that an attorney at a deposition hears voice inflections and sees facial expressions during testimony. These items do not make it onto the transcript, but they are just about as important as the transcribed words. That's why if you change attorneys in midstream, you lose a lot of knowledge. During the short 3 1/2 years of our case, *both* of our attorneys were stricken with potentially fatal illnesses. Both of them! The thought of losing either one was traumatic because besides being the mainstay of our defense, they were both personal friends. Yet neither one missed any depositions, hearings, or meetings.

Thankfully, both fully recovered from their medical emergencies and are as good as new today. I, however, still suffer from chest pain, shortness of breath, and rapid heartbeat whenever I recall these events. It was an interesting 3 1/2 years, but I would not do it again!

If you encounter a sexual harassment suit, keep your head up. Have faith in your friends and attorneys. Keep in mind that potential accusers are still out there. They may knock on your door or come to work for you. Keep your guard up!

Who won? The bean counter at the insurance company, the girl, us, the lawyers? I feel that we won. We did not spend any of our money (OK, I did spend $10 on parking and $1.75 for a hot dog from a street vendor at the courthouse), we were released from the suit, and we could lead normal lives and pursue our fortunes again. God bless America!

Glossary

Feminazi. A word made famous by a large radio and TV talk show host. The definition is very simple— feminists and the Nazis of World War II both had the same basic idea: deprive other groups of their basic freedoms.

Feminist. The term would lead you to visualize a feminine, petite little girl. In all reality, you will probably never, ever, in your entire life see a feminine feminist! The members of this gang are man haters, as unfeminine as can be, and are probably the largest buyers of combat boots other than the U.S. Army!

Innocent male. The feminazis would like this definition to be the standard: "An oppressive beast; crude, lewd, domineering, selfish, arrogant, fit only for reproductive assistance, and if the scientists get to work in the lab, someday will be unnecessary for that purpose." But the true definition is "A hard-working macho man who made the world what it is today!"

Politically correct. This is called going with the flow, not making waves, etc. You ignore common sense and call firemen "fire people," mailmen "mail people," and manhole covers "worker hole covers."